Jungian Psychology

-

The Comprehensive Guide

by

VIRUTI SHIVAN

Masters in Clinical Psychology
(Major)

"In books, as in life, it's not the size or looks but

the content that matters."

Disclaimer: The information in this book is for general information purposes only and is not professional advice. It's not a replacement for proper training, diagnosis, treatment, or guidance from qualified professionals. Although we've tried to ensure accuracy, there may be errors or omissions, so it's essential to consult experts in the relevant fields and independently verify information when needed.

Introduction

Welcome to a journey into the depths of the human psyche, guided by the remarkable insights of Carl Jung, one of the most influential thinkers in psychology. In "Jungian Psychology: The Comprehensive Guide," we're not just reading about theories; we're embarking on an adventure to understand the intricate layers of the human mind and the mysteries that reside within each of us.

Jungian psychology isn't just a subject; it's a lens through which we can view the world, ourselves, and the complex interactions between the two. As we navigate through this guide, we'll explore the foundational concepts of Jung's theories, such as the collective unconscious, archetypes, and the process of individuation. But this isn't your standard textbook journey. We'll delve into these ideas with a sense of wonder, connecting them to everyday experiences, pop culture, and even personal anecdotes where relevant.

Imagine understanding the characters in your favorite movies not just as fictional entities but as representations of universal archetypes that reside within all of us. Think of the dreams you had last night not just as random neural firings but as meaningful narratives woven from the depths of your unconscious. That's the power of Jungian psychology – it turns the ordinary into something extraordinary.

Each chapter in this guide is designed to be engaging and informative, with a touch of human warmth. We'll not only learn about Jung's theories but also how they apply to real life, from our relationships and work to our personal growth and creative expressions. Plus, we're including exercises – like multiple-choice questions at the end of each chapter – to help solidify your understanding and make the learning process interactive and enjoyable.

So, whether you're a student, a professional, or simply curious about the inner workings of the mind, this guide is tailored for you. It's not just about learning; it's about experiencing the world of Jungian psychology. Let's start this fascinating journey together, exploring the depths of the psyche and perhaps, in the process, discovering more about ourselves.

Chapter 1: The Life and Times of Carl Jung

1.1 Early Life and Education

Dive into the early years of Carl Jung, a period that shaped the mind of a man who would later revolutionize the world of psychology. Born in 1875 in Kesswil, Switzerland, Jung's journey began in a quaint village, set against the backdrop of picturesque landscapes—a setting almost symbolic of the inner explorations he would later undertake.

Young Carl was a solitary child, often immersed in his world of thoughts. This introspection was a seed that would eventually grow into his deep understanding of the human psyche. His father, a pastor, and his mother, a keen spiritualist, provided a diverse spiritual and intellectual environment, fueling his curiosity about the human mind and spirit.

As Jung grew, his thirst for knowledge took him to the University of Basel. Here, he delved into medicine, but his passion for psychiatry soon became apparent. It was the late 19th century, and psychiatry was just emerging as a field. Imagine a young, eager Jung, sitting in dimly lit lecture halls, his mind racing with ideas and questions about the human mind.

During his time at university, Jung's interests were eclectic. He was not just confined to medicine and psychiatry; he ventured into philosophy, religion, and literature. This broad spectrum of interests wasn't a mere coincidence. It laid the groundwork for his later work, where he seamlessly integrated concepts from various disciplines into his psychological theories.

Jung's early life was not without challenges. He grappled with personal struggles, including periods of isolation and introspection, which he later recognized as pivotal in his psychological development. These experiences were not just hurdles; they were stepping stones, leading him towards a deeper understanding of the inner world.

Jung's education was not merely academic. It was a journey of personal transformation, setting the stage for his later explorations into the human psyche. His early life was the canvas on which the rest of his career would be painted, rich with experiences, thoughts, and questions that would fuel his groundbreaking work.

As we turn the pages of Jung's early life, we're not just reading a biography; we're witnessing the formation of a mind that would later delve deep into the mysteries of the unconscious, dreams, and the very essence of what it means to be human.

1.2 Jung's Relationship with Freud

The relationship between Carl Jung and Sigmund Freud is a saga of intellectual companionship, eventual discord, and lasting impact. It's a story that reads like a classic drama, brimming with ideas, conflicts, and a profound influence on the course of psychological thought.

In 1907, Jung and Freud met for the first time in Vienna. Picture this: two of the greatest minds in psychology, coming together in an encounter that would change the course of their lives and the field of psychoanalysis. Their first conversation was so captivating that it reportedly lasted for over 13 hours. This meeting of minds was not just a discussion; it was the beginning of a deep intellectual bond.

Jung was initially an ardent supporter of Freud's theories. Freud, in turn, saw in Jung a potential heir to psychoanalysis—a torchbearer for the next generation. Their early collaboration was a period of rich intellectual exchange. They explored the depths of the unconscious, dream analysis, and the dynamics of the psyche.

However, as with many great collaborations, differences soon emerged. Jung began to develop his own ideas, which diverged significantly from Freud's. One of the central points of contention was their differing views on the nature of the unconscious. Freud's perspective was firmly rooted in the idea of repressed desires and sexuality. Jung, on the other hand, introduced the concept of a collective unconscious—a shared repository of human experiences and archetypes.

The divergence wasn't just intellectual; it was personal too. The once warm relationship cooled, as both men defended their respective viewpoints. In 1913, their paths finally parted, marking the end of a significant chapter in the history of psychology. This split was not just between two individuals; it symbolized a branching of psychoanalytic theory into different schools of thought.

Yet, despite the eventual rift, the relationship between Jung and Freud was a catalyst for some of the most important ideas in psychology. It pushed both men to further develop and refine their theories. Jung's break from Freud propelled him to explore new territories in psychology, leading to the development of analytical psychology.

In retrospect, their relationship is a testament to the power of intellectual exchange and the importance of differing viewpoints in the evolution of ideas. The Jung-Freud saga teaches us that from disagreement and debate can emerge some of the most profound insights into the human mind.

1.3 Later Years and Legacy

As we venture into the later years of Carl Jung's life, we enter a period marked by profound introspection, prolific writing, and the solidification of his legacy in the world of psychology.

After his split with Freud, Jung embarked on a period of self-exploration, often referring to it as his "confrontation with the unconscious." This phase was both tumultuous and transformative, leading him to some of his most significant insights. He delved deep into the realms of dreams, symbols, and archetypes, enriching his understanding of the psyche. It was during this time that he developed key concepts such as the collective unconscious and individuation.

Jung's later years were also marked by a prolific output of writing. His works, including "Psychological Types," "The Archetypes and the Collective Unconscious," and "Man and His Symbols," are not just texts but treasure troves of psychological insight. These writings are not mere academic exercises; they read like explorations into the human soul, offering readers a map to navigate the complex terrain of the psyche.

But Jung's impact wasn't confined to the written word. He was also a mentor and teacher, shaping the minds of future psychologists and thinkers. His ideas spawned a new school of thought in psychology—analytical psychology—which continues to influence therapy, counseling, and understanding of the human mind.

Jung's contributions went beyond psychology. He explored the intersections between psychology and other fields such as religion, alchemy, and art, showcasing his belief in the interconnectedness of human experience. His thoughts on synchronicity, the meaningful coincidences in life, offered a new way of looking at the connectedness of events.

As we reflect on Jung's later years, we also witness the growth of his stature as a thinker. He became a respected figure, not just within psychology but in the wider intellectual community. His ideas resonated with people seeking to understand the deeper aspects of existence and their own inner worlds.

Jung's legacy is vast and multifaceted. He left behind not just a body of work, but a lens through which we can view ourselves and our place in the world. His concepts of the shadow, the anima and animus, and the process of individuation are tools that continue to help individuals on their journey towards self-realization.

The story of Carl Jung's later years and legacy is not just a tale of a psychologist's life; it's a narrative about a journey to the depths of the human spirit. His life's work remains a beacon for those navigating the complexities of the psyche, making Carl Jung a timeless figure in the exploration of the human mind.

1.4 Exercise: 10 MCQs with Answers at the End

1. **What year was Carl Jung born?**

   A. 1871

   B. 1875

   C. 1880

   D. 1885

2. **Which university did Carl Jung attend?**

   A. University of Vienna

   B. University of Basel

   C. University of Zurich

   D. University of Munich

3. **Jung's relationship with Freud was initially characterized by:**

   A. Mutual admiration and collaboration

   B. Immediate rivalry and disagreement

   C. Indifference and lack of communication

   D. Mentorship from Freud to Jung

4. What concept is Jung NOT known for?

A. Collective Unconscious

B. Oedipus Complex

C. Archetypes

D. Individuation

5. In which area did Jung and Freud have their most significant disagreement?

A. The role of dreams

B. The nature of the unconscious

C. The importance of childhood experiences

D. The methodology of psychoanalysis

6. What was a major influence on Jung's early life?

A. His father's scientific background

B. His mother's spiritualist tendencies

C. Exposure to diverse cultures

D. Early academic success

7. **Which field did Jung integrate into his psychological theories?**

   A. Mathematics

   B. Philosophy

   C. Chemistry

   D. Biology

8. **What was the title of one of Jung's significant works?**

   A. The Interpretation of Dreams

   B. Psychological Types

   C. Civilization and Its Discontents

   D. Beyond the Pleasure Principle

9. **Jung's concept of 'Individuation' refers to:**

   A. The unconscious influence on behavior

   B. The process of personal development and self-realization

   C. A method of dream analysis

   D. The classification of psychological types

10. **Which concept did Jung NOT explore in his later years?**

A. Alchemy

B. Synchronicity

C. Electra complex

D. Archetypes and symbols

Answers

1. **B. 1875**

2. **B. University of Basel**

3. **A. Mutual admiration and collaboration**

4. **B. Oedipus Complex**

5. **B. The nature of the unconscious**

6. **B. His mother's spiritualist tendencies**

7. **B. Philosophy**

8. **B. Psychological Types**

9. **B. The process of personal development and self-realization**

10. **C. Electra complex**

Chapter 2: The Foundations of Jungian Psychology

2.1 The Psyche and Consciousness

Embarking on the journey through the foundations of Jungian Psychology, we begin with the cornerstone concepts of the psyche and consciousness. These are not just terms; they are the windows through which Carl Jung invites us to view the human mind and its intricate workings.

The Psyche: Think of the psyche as the total personality, a vast, invisible landscape that encompasses everything we are — conscious and unconscious. In Jung's view, it's the epicenter of thought, feeling, and behavior, the command center from which we navigate our lives. It's not just a part of who we are; it is who we are.

Consciousness: This is the part of our psyche that we're aware of, the tip of the iceberg. It's our thoughts, memories, feelings, and sensations that we can identify and articulate. But Jung didn't just see consciousness as a container of thoughts; he saw it as an active process, a dynamic interplay between what we know and what we are yet to discover about ourselves.

Jung's exploration of consciousness wasn't just a clinical study; it was a philosophical quest. He saw consciousness as a lens through which we perceive reality, but also as a barrier limiting our understanding of the broader aspects of the psyche. For Jung, expanding consciousness wasn't just about self-awareness; it was about connecting with the deeper, often overlooked parts of ourselves.

But here's where it gets even more interesting. Jung posited that our consciousness is not a solitary entity but is deeply influenced by the unconscious. This relationship is not just a one-way street; it's a busy intersection where conscious thoughts and unconscious influences meet, mingle, and sometimes collide. This interaction shapes our personality, our choices, and our understanding of ourselves.

In Jungian psychology, the journey of understanding the psyche and consciousness is akin to an adventure into an uncharted territory. It's about exploring the known and venturing into the unknown, discovering hidden treasures of insight and wisdom about ourselves. It's not just a path to self-knowledge; it's a pathway to personal growth and transformation.

So, as we delve deeper into these fundamental concepts, remember that we're not just learning theories; we're embarking on a personal exploration, one that promises to reveal as much about ourselves as it does about the enigmatic mind of Carl Jung.

2.2 The Personal and Collective Unconscious

In the realm of Jungian psychology, the concepts of the personal and collective unconscious form the bedrock of Carl Jung's revolutionary ideas. These aren't just theoretical constructs; they are like hidden worlds within us, shaping our thoughts, behaviors, and experiences in profound ways.

The Personal Unconscious: Imagine this as a personal storage space, a repository of all your repressed memories, forgotten experiences, and undeveloped ideas. It's a private library of feelings, thoughts, and desires that are unique to you but not actively present in your conscious mind. The contents of the personal unconscious include complexes – emotionally charged themes and memories that have a powerful influence on our behavior and outlook.

Jung viewed the personal unconscious as a dynamic part of our psyche, constantly interacting with our conscious mind. It's like a shadow that follows us, invisible yet ever-present, influencing our actions and reactions in ways we might not even be aware of.

The Collective Unconscious: Now, let's take a step further into the depths of the mind, into the collective unconscious. This is not personal; it's universal, a shared heritage of humankind. It's an ancestral memory bank containing the experiences and knowledge of our entire species.

The collective unconscious is home to archetypes – universal, mythic characters or themes that reside within all of us. These archetypes are like psychological DNA, shared patterns of thought and behavior that transcend culture and time. They manifest in our dreams, myths, and stories, representing fundamental human experiences such as the Mother, the Hero, the Trickster, and the Journey.

Jung's concept of the collective unconscious challenges us to think beyond our individual experiences. It suggests that beneath our personal stories lies a deeper narrative, a universal story written in the language of archetypes. This concept invites us to connect with others not just as individuals but as part of a larger, shared human journey.

The dance between the personal and collective unconscious shapes much of our psychological world. It's a dynamic interplay that influences how we perceive ourselves and the world around us. In understanding these aspects of the unconscious, we begin to unravel the complex tapestry of the human psyche, discovering patterns and themes that connect us to each other and to the generations that came before us.

So, as we explore these hidden dimensions of our minds, we're not just uncovering personal secrets; we're tapping into the shared wisdom of humanity. It's a journey that promises to enlighten, challenge, and transform our understanding of ourselves and our place in the world.

2.3 The Ego, Persona, and Shadow

In the vibrant tapestry of Jungian psychology, the concepts of the Ego, Persona, and Shadow are akin to crucial characters in a play, each with a distinct role in the drama of the psyche. Understanding these elements is not just about grasping theoretical ideas; it's about uncovering the layers of our own identity.

The Ego: Picture the Ego as the captain of your psychological ship. It's the center of your conscious awareness, the "I" that you identify as yourself. The Ego is responsible for your feelings of identity and continuity. It's the part of you that navigates the everyday world, making decisions, solving problems, and interacting with others.

But the Ego is more than just a decision-maker; it's a mediator between your inner world and external reality. It balances the demands of the unconscious with the realities of the external world. Think of it as a translator, constantly interpreting the messages from your inner self and finding a way to express them in the outer world.

The Persona: Now, let's meet the Persona, your psychological wardrobe. The Persona is the mask you wear in public, the social face you present to the world. It's the role you play in society — the friendly neighbor, the dedicated employee, the caring friend. The Persona is adaptive; it helps you fit in and function in social situations.

But beware, the Persona can be a double-edged sword. While it helps in social adaptation, over-identification with the Persona can lead to a loss of true self-identity. It's like wearing a mask so long that you forget what's beneath it. Jung warned against letting the Persona dominate, as it can distance you from your authentic self.

The Shadow: In the depths of the psyche lurks the Shadow, the hidden, repressed, and often darker side of your personality. It's the part of you that you don't want to acknowledge – the fears, desires, and impulses that you hide from yourself and others. The Shadow is not just about negative traits; it also holds latent talents and potentials.

Engaging with the Shadow is not for the faint-hearted. It requires you to confront parts of yourself that you might find uncomfortable or embarrassing. But this confrontation is vital. Recognizing and integrating the Shadow is key to achieving psychological balance and wholeness. It's about embracing all parts of yourself, even the ones you'd rather not see.

Together, the Ego, Persona, and Shadow form a dynamic trio that shapes your personality and behavior. They interact in complex ways, influencing how you see yourself and how you relate to the world. Understanding these aspects of your psyche is like getting to know the characters that play out the story of your life. It's a journey of self-discovery, one that leads to a deeper, more holistic understanding of who you are.

2.4 Exercise: 10 MCQs with Answers at the End

1. What is the primary role of the Ego in Jungian psychology?

A. To repress undesirable emotions

B. To navigate the everyday world and make decisions

C. To act as the personal unconscious

D. To connect with the collective unconscious

2. The Persona in Jungian psychology is best described as:

A. The true self

B. The social mask or role one presents to the world

C. The source of creativity

D. The center of consciousness

3. Which of the following is NOT a component of the collective unconscious?

A. Archetypes

B. Personal memories

C. Universal symbols

D. Shared human experiences

4. The Shadow in Jungian psychology represents:

A. The conscious awareness of self

B. The totality of the unconscious

C. The hidden, repressed side of one's personality

D. The external persona presented to society

5. Jung's concept of individuation primarily involves:

A. Strengthening the Ego

B. Suppressing the Shadow

C. Integrating various aspects of the self

D. Focusing on the Persona

6. In Jungian psychology, complexes are mostly associated with:

A. The Ego

B. The Persona

C. The personal unconscious

D. The collective unconscious

7. Archetypes are:

A. Conscious decisions made by the Ego

B. Personal experiences unique to the individual

C. Universal, mythic characters or themes in the collective unconscious

D. Strategies developed by the Persona

8. **An over-identification with the Persona can lead to:**

A. Increased creativity

B. Loss of true self-identity

C. A stronger connection with the collective unconscious

D. Better decision-making skills

9. **The process of confronting and integrating the Shadow is important for:**

A. Maintaining the stability of the Ego

B. Achieving psychological balance and wholeness

C. Enhancing the role of the Persona

D. Suppressing negative traits

10. **Jung's theory of the psyche emphasizes:**

A. The dominance of the conscious mind

B. The separation of personal and collective experiences

C. The interplay between various conscious and unconscious elements

D. The singular importance of the Ego

Answers

1. **B. To navigate the everyday world and make decisions**

2. **B. The social mask or role one presents to the world**

3. **B. Personal memories**

4. **C. The hidden, repressed side of one's personality**

5. **C. Integrating various aspects of the self**

6. **C. The personal unconscious**

7. **C. Universal, mythic characters or themes in the collective unconscious**

8. **B. Loss of true self-identity**

9. **B. Achieving psychological balance and wholeness**

10. **C. The interplay between various conscious and unconscious elements**

Chapter 3: Archetypes and the Collective Unconscious

3.1 Understanding Archetypes

In the captivating landscape of Jungian psychology, archetypes stand as towering, enigmatic figures. To understand archetypes is to delve into the universal language of the human psyche, a language that transcends time, culture, and personal experience.

What are Archetypes? Imagine archetypes as the original blueprints of human thoughts and behaviors, deeply embedded in the collective unconscious. They are not specific characters or images, but rather patterns or themes that recur across different cultures and times. Archetypes are like the DNA of our psychological makeup, forming the substratum of our collective psychological inheritance.

The Universal Nature of Archetypes: The beauty of archetypes lies in their universality. From the myths of ancient Greece to modern-day movies, from the rituals of indigenous tribes to the novels on your bookshelf, archetypes permeate human expression. They are the common threads that weave through the tapestry of human experience, revealing shared dreams, fears, passions, and aspirations.

Examples of Archetypes: Jung identified several key archetypes, each representing fundamental human experiences. The 'Mother' archetype embodies nurturing, caring, and birth. The 'Hero' represents bravery, adventure, and the quest for self-discovery. The 'Trickster' embodies mischief, cunning, and the disruption of the status quo. These are not just characters; they are echoes of our deepest human instincts and experiences.

Archetypes in Dreams and Art: Dreams are a canvas on which these archetypes often paint their stories. In the realm of dreams, archetypes manifest as symbolic figures or situations that carry a wealth of meaning. Similarly, art, literature, and folklore are rich repositories of archetypal images and narratives, offering insights into the collective human psyche.

Why Understanding Archetypes Matters: Engaging with archetypes is not just an academic exercise; it's a journey into the heart of what it means to be human. By understanding archetypes, we gain insight into our own lives and the collective experiences of humanity. They help us to comprehend the patterns of our behavior, our relationships, and our place in the world.

Archetypes, in essence, are the storytellers of the human soul, narrating tales as old as humanity itself. As we explore these timeless patterns, we are not just learning about abstract concepts; we are uncovering the shared narrative of the human journey, a journey that each of us is a part of.

3.2 Major Archetypes: Anima/Animus, Shadow, Self

Jungian psychology is a treasure trove of profound concepts, and among these, the archetypes of Anima/Animus, Shadow, and Self are particularly pivotal. These are not just theoretical constructs; they are vital keys to unlocking a deeper understanding of our psyche and our journey towards self-realization.

Anima and Animus: The Anima and Animus represent the feminine and masculine energies present within each individual, regardless of gender. Think of them as the yin and yang of your personality. The Anima is the feminine aspect residing in the unconscious of men, while the Animus is the masculine aspect in women.

These archetypes play a crucial role in how we relate to the opposite sex and our internal balance. The Anima/Animus influences our romantic choices, our creativity, and even our life goals. When we engage with these archetypes, we tap into a wellspring of insights about our relationships and our inner balance of masculine and feminine energies.

The Shadow: If the Anima/Animus are the dancers, the Shadow is the dance floor, often hidden in the dark. The Shadow is the part of ourselves we often try to hide or deny – those aspects we consider to be weak, shameful, or frightening. It's the reservoir of repressed thoughts, feelings, and desires.

The journey of integrating the Shadow is about acknowledging and embracing these hidden parts of ourselves. It's not about eradicating them but understanding their role in our psychological makeup. Confronting the Shadow can be challenging, but it's essential for achieving wholeness and authenticity.

The Self: The Self is the grand orchestrator of the psyche, representing the unity and totality of the individual. It's the archetype of wholeness and the goal of the process of individuation – the journey towards integrating all aspects of one's personality.

The Self is not just the sum of our parts; it's the realization of our fullest potential. It's the guiding force that leads us towards a balanced and harmonious existence, helping us to reconcile the various conflicting aspects of our personality.

In understanding these major archetypes – Anima/Animus, Shadow, and Self – we gain a richer, more nuanced understanding of ourselves and our journey towards psychological growth. They are not just concepts; they are mirrors reflecting the diverse facets of our being, guiding us towards a deeper, more integrated understanding of who we are and who we can become.

3.3 Archetypes and Mythology

In the vibrant narrative of Jungian psychology, the relationship between archetypes and mythology is like a dance between ancient stories and modern minds. This connection offers a fascinating lens through which we can view the timeless tales that have shaped human culture and consciousness.

Mythology: A Canvas for Archetypes: Mythology, in all its colorful and varied forms, is essentially a gallery of archetypes in action. These myths, legends, and folktales from diverse cultures are not just stories; they are reflections of the collective unconscious, showcasing universal patterns and themes that resonate across time and space.

Archetypes as Mythological Characters: In myths, archetypes manifest as gods, goddesses, heroes, and villains – each embodying essential aspects of the human experience. For instance, the Greek god Zeus represents the archetype of the Father – a symbol of authority and power. The Hero's journey, a common theme in many myths, echoes the archetype of the Hero, illustrating the quest for self-discovery and transformation.

Understanding Ourselves Through Myths: Myths are more than ancient tales; they are tools for understanding our own lives. They provide a framework for understanding our struggles, aspirations, and journeys. By identifying with mythological characters and themes, we connect with the archetypes within us, gaining insights into our own psyche and life patterns.

The Universal Language of Mythology: Mythology speaks a universal language that transcends cultural and historical boundaries. It taps into the collective unconscious, drawing upon shared human experiences and emotions. This universality makes mythology a powerful medium for understanding the human condition and the archetypal forces that shape our lives.

Modern Myths and Archetypes: The influence of archetypes and mythology is not confined to ancient stories. Modern narratives, whether in literature, film, or other art forms, continue to draw upon these timeless themes. Characters like the misunderstood outsider or the reluctant hero are modern expressions of archetypal patterns, illustrating their enduring relevance.

In exploring the interplay between archetypes and mythology, we are not just studying old stories; we are uncovering the narrative threads that weave through the human psyche. Myths offer a map to navigate the landscape of our inner world, revealing truths about ourselves and the universal human journey we all share.

3.4 Exercise: 10 MCQs with Answers at the End

1. **Which archetype represents the feminine aspect in the unconscious of men, according to Jung?**

   A. Shadow

   B. Anima

   C. Animus

   D. Hero

2. **The archetype of the 'Mother' typically embodies:**

   A. Adventure and bravery

   B. Nurturing and caring

   C. Mischief and cunning

   D. Authority and power

3. **In Jungian psychology, the 'Self' is:**

   A. The center of conscious awareness

   B. The hidden, repressed part of the psyche

   C. The archetype of wholeness and the goal of individuation

   D. The social mask presented to the world

4. The 'Hero's Journey' in mythology corresponds to which Jungian archetype?

A. The Shadow

B. The Anima

C. The Self

D. The Hero

5. What role does mythology play in understanding archetypes?

A. It provides historical accuracy for psychological theories

B. It serves as a reflection of the collective unconscious

C. It is unrelated to archetypal patterns

D. It offers a scientific explanation of human behavior

6. Which archetype is known for embodying the darker, repressed side of one's personality?

A. The Mother

B. The Shadow

C. The Hero

D. The Anima

7. **The Animus represents:**

A. The masculine aspect in the unconscious of men

B. The feminine aspect in the unconscious of women

C. The masculine aspect in the unconscious of women

D. The social role of men in society

8. **Archetypes in Jungian psychology are:**

A. Personal memories and experiences unique to the individual

B. Universal, mythic patterns in the collective unconscious

C. Conscious decisions made by the Ego

D. Strategies developed by the Persona

9. **The concept of the 'Trickster' in mythology typically represents:**

A. Authority and discipline

B. Creativity and transformation

C. Nurturing and protection

D. Mischief and disruption of the status quo

10. **Integrating the Shadow into one's personality is important for:**

   A. Enhancing the role of the Persona

   B. Achieving psychological balance and wholeness

   C. Suppressing negative traits

   D. Maintaining the stability of the Ego

Answers

1. **B. Anima**

2. **B. Nurturing and caring**

3. **C. The archetype of wholeness and the goal of individuation**

4. **D. The Hero**

5. **B. It serves as a reflection of the collective unconscious**

6. **B. The Shadow**

7. **C. The masculine aspect in the unconscious of women**

8. **B. Universal, mythic patterns in the collective unconscious**

9. **D. Mischief and disruption of the status quo**

10. **B. Achieving psychological balance and wholeness**

Chapter 4: The Process of Individuation

4.1 The Journey to Self-Discovery

Embarking on the process of individuation in Jungian psychology is like setting sail on a grand voyage of self-discovery. This journey is at the heart of Carl Jung's work, a path leading to the harmonious integration of the conscious and unconscious aspects of the self.

Understanding Individuation: Individuation is not a mere psychological concept; it's a deeply personal process of becoming aware of and reconciling the different parts of one's personality. It's about becoming who you truly are – a unique individual, distinct from societal and familial expectations and influences.

The Phases of the Journey: This journey typically unfolds in various stages, beginning with the confrontation with the Shadow, where one faces the darker, repressed aspects of the self. It involves recognizing and integrating the Anima/Animus, balancing the masculine and feminine aspects within. As the journey progresses, the Persona – the social mask – is examined and its influence on the self is understood.

The Role of Dreams and Symbols: In this process, dreams and symbols serve as vital guides. They are the language of the unconscious, offering insights and messages that help in understanding and integrating the various aspects of the psyche. Jung saw dreams as direct expressions of the unconscious, rich with symbolic meaning pointing towards the areas of the self that need attention and integration.

The Goal of Wholeness: The ultimate aim of individuation is not perfection, but wholeness. It's about embracing all aspects of oneself, including those that are often hidden or ignored. This process leads to a more balanced, integrated, and authentic self.

Personal Growth and Transformation: Individuation is inherently transformative. It's a journey that challenges, enlightens, and changes a person. As one delves deeper into understanding the self, there is a profound personal growth that transcends the boundaries of conventional psychological theories.

A Lifelong Journey: Individuation is not a destination but a lifelong journey. It's a continuous process of self-exploration and self-realization, where each step brings greater self-awareness and a deeper connection to the self and the world.

Embarking on the journey to self-discovery through the process of individuation is like unlocking a treasure trove of personal insights and potentials. It's a voyage that offers the promise of a more authentic, integrated, and fulfilling life, a journey that reveals the true essence of who you are and who you can become.

4.2 Stages of Individuation

The process of individuation in Jungian psychology is a fascinating journey with distinct stages, each representing a significant step in the journey towards self-realization and wholeness. These stages are not linear checkpoints but rather phases of a spiraling journey of personal growth and understanding.

1. Confrontation with the Shadow: This initial stage involves facing the darker, often neglected parts of the self – the Shadow. It's about recognizing and acknowledging the repressed, hidden aspects of one's personality. This confrontation is often challenging, as it requires accepting traits and impulses that one might find uncomfortable or undesirable. However, integrating the Shadow is crucial for achieving a more complete understanding of the self.

2. Encounter with the Anima/Animus: The next stage involves engaging with the Anima or Animus – the feminine aspect in men and the masculine aspect in women. This encounter helps to balance the masculine and feminine energies within the individual, leading to a richer, more nuanced understanding of the self and the opposite sex. It often manifests in dreams, fantasies, and projections onto others.

3. The Realization of the Persona: In this stage, individuals become aware of their Persona – the social mask they wear in different situations. This realization involves understanding how this mask influences behavior and interactions and may not fully represent the true self. It's about differentiating between the roles one plays and one's authentic identity.

4. Integration of the Self: The final stage is the integration of the Self, where the individual begins to unify the various aspects of their personality. This stage is marked by a sense of wholeness and balance. The Self in Jungian terms represents the center of the personality, a unifying force that harmonizes the conscious and unconscious, the Ego, Shadow, Anima/Animus, and Persona.

5. Living the Process: Individuation is a dynamic, ongoing process. It's not just about reaching a state of balance but maintaining and living it. This stage is about continuously applying the insights gained from the journey to everyday life, leading to ongoing personal growth, creativity, and psychological resilience.

Each stage of individuation is a step towards a deeper understanding and acceptance of oneself. It's a journey that not only reveals the complexities of the psyche but also offers a path to a more authentic and fulfilling life. Through this process, individuals can transcend beyond their perceived limitations and discover their true potential.

4.3 Challenges and Transformations

The journey of individuation in Jungian psychology, while deeply rewarding, is laden with challenges and transformative experiences. These hurdles and changes are not merely obstacles; they are integral to the process of achieving personal growth and self-awareness.

Confronting the Uncomfortable: One of the first and perhaps most daunting challenges is confronting aspects of the self that have been repressed or ignored – particularly the Shadow. This confrontation often brings to the surface uncomfortable truths about ourselves, fears, and desires that we have hidden away. It requires a great deal of courage and honesty to face these hidden aspects, but it is essential for true self-understanding.

Balancing the Anima/Animus: Engaging with the Anima or Animus presents its own set of challenges. It involves recognizing and integrating the feminine or masculine aspects of the self, which can be a complex and confusing process. For many, this means exploring parts of their identity that they may have never consciously acknowledged or understood before.

Redefining the Persona: Another significant challenge is redefining and understanding the role of the Persona – the social mask we wear. People often struggle with differentiating their true self from the roles they play in society. This challenge is about finding a balance between adapting to social norms and staying true to one's authentic self.

Experiencing Transformation: Each challenge in the journey of individuation is accompanied by transformation. As individuals confront and integrate aspects of their Shadow, Anima/Animus, and Persona, they undergo profound changes in their self-perception and worldview.

Psychological Resilience: The process of individuation fosters psychological resilience. As one navigates through these challenges, there's an increasing ability to cope with stress, change, and adversity. This resilience is a byproduct of facing and integrating the complexities of the self.

Enhanced Relationships and Creativity: The transformations that occur during individuation often lead to healthier relationships and enhanced creativity. By understanding themselves better, individuals can relate to others more authentically and express themselves more freely and creatively.

Continual Growth: It's important to remember that individuation is not a one-time event but a continuous process. The challenges and transformations experienced are not endpoints but milestones in an ongoing journey of self-discovery and development.

In essence, the challenges and transformations inherent in the process of individuation are opportunities for profound personal growth. They offer a pathway to a more authentic, balanced, and fulfilling life, allowing individuals to tap into their deepest potentials and live with greater awareness and creativity.

4.4 Exercise: 10 MCQs with Answers at the End

1. The process of individuation in Jungian psychology primarily aims to:

A. Eliminate the unconscious

B. Achieve a balanced and integrated personality

C. Focus solely on enhancing the Ego

D. Repress the Shadow

2. The first stage of individuation involves:

A. Realizing the Persona

B. Integrating the Self

C. Confronting the Shadow

D. Encountering the Anima/Animus

3. Integrating the Anima/Animus archetype is crucial for:

A. Balancing masculine and feminine aspects within an individual

B. Strengthening the Ego

C. Eliminating the Persona

D. Suppressing unconscious desires

4. In the process of individuation, the Persona is:

A. Integrated as the central part of the personality

B. Recognized and understood in its influence on the self

C. Completely discarded

D. The main focus of psychological analysis

5. Which stage of individuation is marked by a sense of wholeness and balance?

A. Confrontation with the Shadow

B. Encounter with the Anima/Animus

C. Realization of the Persona

D. Integration of the Self

6. The process of individuation leads to:

A. A less complex understanding of the self

B. Psychological resilience and personal growth

C. Weakening of personal relationships

D. A static state of being

7. **Confronting the Shadow can often bring to the surface:**

   A. Only negative traits and impulses

   B. Uncomfortable truths and repressed aspects of the self

   C. The true purpose of the Persona

   D. A simplified view of the personality

8. **During individuation, encountering the Anima/Animus influences:**

   A. Only romantic relationships

   B. Creativity and life goals

   C. Social status

   D. Professional achievements

9. **Individuation is considered:**

   A. A one-time event

   B. A continuous, lifelong process

   C. Only relevant in therapy

   D. Unrelated to personal relationships

10. **The ultimate aim of individuation is:**

   A. Perfection

   B. Wholeness

   C. Social conformity

D. Dominance of the Ego

Answers

1. **B. Achieve a balanced and integrated personality**

2. **C. Confronting the Shadow**

3. **A. Balancing masculine and feminine aspects within an individual**

4. **B. Recognized and understood in its influence on the self**

5. **D. Integration of the Self**

6. **B. Psychological resilience and personal growth**

7. **B. Uncomfortable truths and repressed aspects of the self**

8. **B. Creativity and life goals**

9. **B. A continuous, lifelong process**

10. **B. Wholeness**

Chapter 5: Dreams and Their Interpretation

5.1 The Role of Dreams in Jungian Psychology

In the captivating narrative of Jungian psychology, dreams hold a place of paramount importance. Far from being mere nocturnal reveries, dreams are viewed as vital communications from the depths of the unconscious, rich in symbolic meaning and insights into the self.

Dreams as a Gateway to the Unconscious: Jung considered dreams as the most direct expressions of the unconscious, offering a window into the parts of ourselves that lie beyond our conscious awareness. They are like messages in a bottle, sent from the depths of our psyche, containing valuable information about our inner world.

Symbolic Language of Dreams: Dreams communicate in the language of symbols. These symbols are not arbitrary but are deeply personal and often universal in nature. They represent the archetypes of the collective unconscious, manifesting in forms and narratives that are unique to each individual's experiences and psychological makeup.

Function of Dreams in Psychological Development: Dreams, in Jungian psychology, serve a compensatory function. They often reveal aspects of ourselves that are underdeveloped or ignored in our waking life. For example, if a person is overly rational, their dreams might be filled with emotional or irrational imagery, urging them to pay attention to their neglected emotional side.

Dreams as a Tool for Individuation: Dreams are instrumental in the process of individuation, guiding the dreamer towards a more balanced and integrated personality. They often present scenarios, characters, and symbols that highlight areas of the psyche that need to be acknowledged, confronted, or integrated.

Working with Dreams in Therapy: In Jungian therapy, dream analysis is a core component. By exploring and interpreting dreams, individuals gain insights into their unconscious motivations, fears, desires, and conflicts. This exploration is not about finding a one-size-fits-all meaning but uncovering the personal significance and message that the dream holds for the dreamer.

A Reflective Mirror: Dreams act as a reflective mirror, showing us not only who we are but also who we might become. They challenge us, comfort us, and sometimes confound us, pushing us to explore the depths of our psyche and embark on a journey of self-discovery.

In Jungian psychology, dreams are not just a footnote; they are a central piece of the puzzle in understanding the human psyche. They invite us to delve into the mysterious and often unexplored territories of our mind, offering a rich tapestry of symbols and meanings that guide us towards psychological wholeness and self-awareness.

5.2 Symbolism in Dreams

In the fascinating world of Jungian psychology, symbolism in dreams is akin to a language of the soul, speaking in metaphors and images that convey deeper meanings and insights. Understanding this symbolism is a key to unlocking the messages our unconscious is trying to communicate.

The Nature of Dream Symbols: Dream symbols are not just random images; they are imbued with personal and universal significance. They are the manifestations of our deepest fears, desires, and questions, often presented in a metaphorical or symbolic language that transcends ordinary verbal communication.

Personal vs. Universal Symbols: Jung distinguished between personal symbols, which are unique to the individual's experience and cultural background, and universal symbols, or archetypes, which are common across different cultures and times. For instance, water might universally symbolize the unconscious, but its personal meaning for a dreamer might vary based on their experiences with water.

Common Archetypal Symbols in Dreams: There are numerous archetypal symbols found in dreams, each carrying its own set of meanings. A few examples include:

  - **The Shadow:** Often appears as a dark figure or an unknown person, representing the unacknowledged parts of the self.

  - **The Anima/Animus:** May manifest as a figure of the opposite sex, embodying the feminine qualities in men (Anima) or the masculine qualities in women (Animus).

  - **The Wise Old Man/Woman:** Symbolizes wisdom, guidance, and insight.

  - **The Trickster:** Often appears as a mischievous character, representing the disruptive side of the personality.

Emotional and Contextual Interpretation: In dream analysis, the emotional context and the personal circumstances of the dreamer are crucial. The same symbol can have different meanings depending on the feelings associated with it in the dream and the current life situation of the dreamer.

Active Imagination and Dream Interpretation: Jung encouraged a technique called active imagination as a way to engage with dream symbols. This involves revisiting the dream while awake and allowing oneself to interact imaginatively with the dream elements, thereby uncovering deeper layers of meaning.

Dreams as a Reflection of the Psyche's Balance: Dreams often symbolically represent the current state of balance (or imbalance) in the psyche. For instance, a dream featuring a chaotic scene might reflect inner turmoil, while a dream of flying might indicate a newfound sense of freedom or escape from constraints.

In Jungian psychology, the symbolism in dreams is a profound and rich source of psychological insight. It's a symbolic language through which the unconscious communicates, offering guidance, revealing inner conflicts, and pointing towards paths for personal growth and self-understanding. Deciphering this language is a journey into the deeper realms of the self, revealing truths that lie beyond the reach of conscious awareness.

5.3 Techniques of Dream Analysis

Dream analysis in Jungian psychology is a meticulous and introspective process, designed to decipher the cryptic messages of our unconscious. It involves various techniques that help individuals connect with the deeper aspects of their psyche through the interpretation of dreams. Let's explore some of these key techniques:

1. Recording the Dream: The first step in dream analysis is to capture the dream as soon as possible after waking up. Keeping a dream journal is essential. The dream should be recorded in as much detail as possible, noting not just the events and characters but also the emotions experienced during the dream.

2. Identifying Symbols and Motifs: Once the dream is recorded, the next step is to identify the symbols and motifs within it. This involves looking for recurring themes, unusual or striking elements, and elements that evoke a strong emotional response. Each symbol in the dream is treated as an important piece of a larger puzzle.

3. Personal Association: This technique involves exploring what each symbol in the dream personally means to the dreamer. Jung believed that the personal context and the dreamer's associations with each symbol are crucial for understanding the dream's meaning. The dreamer might ask, "What does this symbol remind me of?" or "How do I feel about this element in my waking life?"

4. Amplification: Amplification involves expanding upon the personal associations by exploring the cultural, historical, and archetypal meanings of the symbols. This might include researching myths, religious texts, or folklore to find broader meanings and connections.

5. Active Imagination: This technique, introduced by Jung, involves re-entering the dream while awake and engaging with the dream elements in an imaginative, conscious state. It allows for a dialogue with the unconscious and can lead to new insights and understandings.

6. Understanding the Compensation Theory: Jung believed that dreams often serve to compensate for imbalances in the conscious attitude of the dreamer. Analyzing dreams from this perspective involves asking how the dream might be offering a counterbalance to the dreamer's conscious beliefs, feelings, and behaviors.

7. Consulting with a Jungian Analyst: While personal analysis of dreams is valuable, working with a Jungian analyst can provide additional depth and insight. These professionals are trained in deciphering the complex language of dreams and can guide the dreamer through the interpretative process.

8. Reflecting on the Emotional Response: Finally, it is essential to reflect on the emotional response both within the dream and upon waking. Understanding how one feels about the dream and its elements can provide crucial clues to its meaning.

In Jungian dream analysis, dreams are not just a collection of random images; they are viewed as meaningful expressions of the unconscious mind. The process of analyzing these dreams is both an art and a science, requiring patience, introspection, and a willingness to explore the depths of one's inner world. Through this process, individuals can gain profound insights into their psyche, aiding their journey towards self-understanding and psychological growth.

5.4 Exercise: 10 MCQs with Answers at the End

1. **In Jungian psychology, dreams are primarily viewed as:**

   A. Random neural activities during sleep

   B. Predictions of the future

   C. Messages from the unconscious

   D. Recollections of daily activities

2. **Which technique involves writing down the dream in as much detail as possible?**

   A. Personal Association

   B. Recording the Dream

   C. Active Imagination

   D. Amplification

3. **The process of exploring personal meanings attached to dream symbols is known as:**

   A. Symbol Identification

   B. Active Imagination

   C. Personal Association

D. Compensation Analysis

4. Amplification in dream analysis refers to:

A. Making the dream more vivid and memorable

B. Expanding on symbols by exploring their broader cultural and historical meanings

C. Increasing the emotional intensity of the dream

D. Focusing solely on the most significant symbol in the dream

5. Active Imagination in the context of dream analysis is:

A. Re-imagining the dream while awake to engage with its elements

B. Dreaming intentionally about a specific topic

C. Increasing dream recall ability

D. Analyzing dreams during meditation

6. Jung's theory of Compensation in dreams suggests that they often:

A. Reflect the dreamer's conscious life exactly

B. Serve to balance imbalances in the dreamer's conscious attitude

C. Are completely unrelated to the dreamer's waking life

D. Focus solely on unresolved past traumas

7. Consulting with a Jungian Analyst in dream analysis is beneficial for:

A. Forgetting disturbing dreams

B. Providing an authoritative interpretation of the dream

C. Offering depth and insight in interpreting complex dream symbols

D. Ensuring that all dreams are interpreted as predictions

8. Which of these is a common archetypal symbol in dreams?

A. The Wise Old Man/Woman

B. A specific historical figure

C. A modern technological device

D. A detailed map of a known city

9. Understanding the emotional response in a dream is important for:

A. Dismissing irrelevant dreams

B. Determining the literal meaning of the dream

C. Understanding the dream's impact on the dreamer

D. Changing the dream's narrative in future dreams

10. **The ultimate goal of Jungian dream analysis is to:**

   A. Stop unwanted dreams

   B. Predict future events

   C. Gain insights into the unconscious mind

   D. Improve memory retention

Answers

1. **C. Messages from the unconscious**

2. **B. Recording the Dream**

3. **C. Personal Association**

4. **B. Expanding on symbols by exploring their broader cultural and historical meanings**

5. **A. Re-imagining the dream while awake to engage with its elements**

6. **B. Serve to balance imbalances in the dreamer's conscious attitude**

7. **C. Offering depth and insight in interpreting complex dream symbols**

8. **A. The Wise Old Man/Woman**

9. **C. Understanding the dream's impact on the dreamer**

10. **C. Gain insights into the unconscious mind**

Chapter 6: Psychological Types

6.1 The Four Functions

In Jungian psychology, the concept of psychological types is central to understanding personality. Jung identified four primary functions that are key to how individuals perceive and interact with the world. These functions, two perceptive (or 'irrational') and two judging (or 'rational'), work together in varying degrees in each person, leading to diverse personality types.

1. Sensation: This function is about perceiving through the five senses. Individuals with a dominant sensation function are highly aware of the physical world and their sensory experiences. They tend to focus on the present, on what is real and tangible. They are often practical, detail-oriented, and grounded in reality.

2. Intuition: Intuition is the perceptive function that involves perceiving things beyond what is immediately apparent or tangible. Those who lean toward intuition are more attuned to possibilities, patterns, and abstract ideas. They are often imaginative, future-oriented, and enjoy exploring new concepts and unconventional solutions.

3. Thinking: The thinking function is a judging or rational function. It involves making decisions and judgments based on objective principles and logical reasoning. Thinkers tend to analyze situations logically, value objectivity, and are often skilled at identifying flaws in arguments and systems.

4. Feeling: This is the other judging function, which makes decisions based on subjective values and emotional considerations. Feelers prioritize empathy, harmony, and the impact of decisions on others. They are often sensitive to the needs and feelings of others and value personal connections.

Balancing the Functions: According to Jung, psychological health and maturity involve developing a balance among these functions, with one typically being more dominant. The dominant function characterizes the conscious personality, while the opposite, less developed function resides in the unconscious.

Interplay with Personality: The interplay of these functions contributes to the complexity of personality. For example, an individual who is predominantly intuitive and feeling will have a very different outlook and approach to life compared to someone who is predominantly sensing and thinking.

In understanding these four functions, Jung provided a framework for understanding the diverse ways in which people perceive the world and make decisions. It's a tool that helps in appreciating the richness and complexity of human personality and in recognizing the inherent value in different perspectives and approaches to life.

6.2 Typology and Personality Development

Delving into the realm of Jungian psychology, we find that typology plays a significant role in understanding and developing personality. Jung's typology is not just a system for categorizing people; it's a dynamic framework for exploring the growth and evolution of the individual personality.

Jung's Psychological Types: Jung's concept of psychological types stems from the interplay of the four functions (thinking, feeling, sensation, intuition) and the two attitudes (introversion and extraversion). An individual's type is influenced by the dominant function and attitude, shaping their outlook and approach to life.

Personality Development: In the journey of personal development, understanding one's typology is crucial. It provides insight into natural preferences and inclinations, helping individuals recognize their strengths and areas for growth.

The Role of the Dominant Function: The dominant function strongly influences how an individual interacts with the world.

For instance, a dominant thinker will approach situations logically, while a dominant feeler will prioritize emotional values.

Developing the Inferior Function: Jung emphasized the importance of developing the inferior, or least developed, function for achieving psychological balance. This process often involves confronting aspects of the self that are less comfortable or familiar, leading to a more rounded and integrated personality.

The Balance of Introversion and Extraversion: Jung's typology also considers the balance between introversion (focus on the internal world) and extraversion (focus on the external world). Understanding and balancing these attitudes is key to personal growth, as it affects how individuals engage with their environment and relationships.

Adaptation and Growth: Typology in Jungian psychology is not about pigeonholing individuals into fixed categories. Rather, it's about understanding predispositions and using this knowledge for adaptation and growth. It encourages self-awareness and flexibility in various aspects of life, including career choices, relationships, and personal challenges.

Integration of Opposites: The ultimate goal in Jungian personality development is the integration of opposites – not just the dominant and inferior functions, but also the conscious and unconscious aspects of the self. This integration leads to what Jung referred to as individuation, a process of becoming wholly oneself.

Jung's typology offers a rich and nuanced understanding of personality development. It's a tool for self-discovery and growth, providing a pathway to a more balanced and authentic self. By engaging with our psychological type, we embark on a journey of understanding the complexities of our personality and harnessing our full potential.

6.3 Application in Therapy and Personal Growth

Jung's typology, with its deep insights into personality, finds significant application in both therapy and personal growth. By understanding one's psychological type, individuals can embark on a journey of self-discovery and development that can be transformative.

Application in Therapy:

1. **Self-Awareness and Insight:** In therapy, Jungian typology can be used to help clients gain a deeper understanding of themselves. Knowing one's dominant functions and attitudes (introversion/extraversion) can provide insight into behavioral patterns, relationship dynamics, and life choices.

2. **Addressing Imbalance:** Therapists can use Jung's typology to identify and address imbalances in the psyche. For example, someone with a dominant thinking function might struggle with understanding or expressing emotions, an area where therapy can provide assistance.

3. **Working with the Shadow:** Jungian therapy often involves exploring and integrating the Shadow – the parts of ourselves that we are unaware of or tend to reject. Understanding one's psychological type can help in identifying the qualities that are in the Shadow.

4. **Personal Growth and Individuation:** The ultimate goal of Jungian therapy is individuation, or the process of becoming one's true self. This involves integrating various aspects of the personality, a process that is facilitated by understanding one's typology.

Application in Personal Growth:

1. **Career and Lifestyle Choices:** Knowledge of one's Jungian type can guide career and lifestyle choices that are more aligned with one's natural inclinations and strengths, leading to greater satisfaction and success.

2. **Improving Relationships:** By understanding their typology, individuals can better understand their interaction patterns and improve their relationships. Recognizing differences in types can foster empathy and better communication with others.

3. **Stress Management:** Understanding one's psychological type can be crucial in developing effective stress management strategies. For example, an introverted individual might find solace in solitary activities, while an extravert might relieve stress through social interactions.

4. **Creativity and Problem-Solving:** Jung's typology can enhance creativity and problem-solving skills by encouraging individuals to tap into their less dominant functions and explore different perspectives.

5. **Holistic Development:** Jung's approach encourages a holistic development of the self. By recognizing and developing the less dominant aspects of their personality, individuals can achieve a more balanced and fulfilling life.

In essence, Jung's typology is a powerful tool in therapy and personal growth. It offers a roadmap for understanding oneself and navigating the complexities of life with greater awareness and authenticity. This approach not only fosters personal development but also enriches interactions with the world and others.

6.4 Exercise: 10 MCQs with Answers at the End

1. What are the two main attitudes described in Jung's typology?

A. Sensing and Intuition

B. Thinking and Feeling

C. Introversion and Extraversion

D. Perception and Judgement

2. In Jungian psychology, which function is focused on logical reasoning and objective decision-making?

A. Sensation

B. Intuition

C. Thinking

D. Feeling

3. Which function in Jung's typology is about perceiving through the five senses?

A. Sensation

B. Intuition

C. Thinking

D. Feeling

4. The process of becoming one's true self in Jungian therapy is known as:

A. Compensation

B. Individuation

C. Amplification

D. Assimilation

5. An individual with a dominant Feeling function typically makes decisions based on:

A. Logic and objectivity

B. Emotional responses and values

C. Sensory information

D. Future possibilities

6. The Jungian function that focuses on possibilities, patterns, and abstract ideas is:

A. Sensation

B. Intuition

C. Thinking

D. Feeling

7. In Jung's typology, the balance between different functions and attitudes is important for:

A. Developing psychic abilities

B. Achieving psychological balance and wholeness

C. Increasing intellectual capacity

D. Enhancing physical health

8. The use of Jungian typology in career guidance is primarily to:

A. Predict job performance

B. Align career paths with personality traits

C. Assess skill levels

D. Determine salary expectations

9. In Jungian psychology, integrating the Shadow aspect in therapy helps in:

A. Forgetting past traumas

B. Developing the dominant function

C. Recognizing and accepting repressed parts of oneself

D. Eliminating negative emotions

10. **A person with a dominant Introverted Intuition function is likely to:**

A. Focus on detailed sensory information

B. Engage in objective analysis

C. Be drawn to abstract ideas and future possibilities

D. Base decisions on emotional values

Answers

1. **C. Introversion and Extraversion**

2. **C. Thinking**

3. **A. Sensation**

4. **B. Individuation**

5. **B. Emotional responses and values**

6. **B. Intuition**

7. **B. Achieving psychological balance and wholeness**

8. **B. Align career paths with personality traits**

9. **C. Recognizing and accepting repressed parts of oneself**

10. **C. Be drawn to abstract ideas and future possibilities**

Chapter 7: Symbols and Complexes

7.1 Understanding Symbols in Psychology

In the realm of Jungian psychology, symbols hold a place of significant importance. They are not mere representations or illustrations; they are powerful tools for communicating the deeper aspects of the psyche, bridging the conscious and the unconscious mind.

Nature of Symbols: Symbols in psychology are images, objects, or concepts that represent something beyond their immediate, literal meaning. They often emerge from the unconscious and carry with them a wealth of layered meanings and emotional significance. Symbols are the language through which the deeper and often inarticulable aspects of our psyche communicate with our conscious mind.

Symbols as a Means of Expression: For Jung, symbols were essential in expressing things that are otherwise hard to verbalize. They often appear in dreams, fantasies, and artistic expressions, offering insights into the workings of the inner self. Symbols can be deeply personal (unique to an individual) or universal (shared across cultures and times).

The Role of Symbols in the Unconscious: In Jungian psychology, symbols are seen as manifestations of the unconscious mind. They often appear in response to situations where our conscious mind is unable to process or articulate complex emotional experiences or internal conflicts.

Symbols in Dreams: One of the most common ways symbols manifest is in dreams. In dream analysis, understanding the symbolism is crucial for interpreting the underlying messages and meanings of the dream. These symbols can range from archetypal images common across human experiences to highly personal images that relate to the individual's life.

Cultural and Archetypal Symbols: Jung also emphasized the importance of cultural symbols and myths in understanding the collective unconscious. These archetypal symbols are deeply ingrained in the human psyche and are recurrent in myths, religions, and fairy tales across different cultures.

The Transformative Power of Symbols: Symbols have a transformative power in psychology. Engaging with and understanding one's personal symbols can lead to profound insights and personal growth. They can reveal hidden desires, fears, and aspects of our personality, guiding us towards greater self-awareness and psychological integration.

In summary, symbols in psychology are much more than mere signs or representations. They are dynamic, powerful entities that connect our conscious reality with the mysterious depths of the unconscious. Understanding and interpreting these symbols is a key aspect of the journey towards self-knowledge and psychological maturity in Jungian therapy.

7.2 Major Complexes and Their Impacts

In Jungian psychology, complexes are key elements that significantly impact an individual's psyche and behavior. These complexes are clusters of emotions, memories, perceptions, and wishes in the unconscious, organized around a common theme.

Understanding Complexes: A complex is like an emotional knot in the psyche, often unconscious, that influences thoughts and behaviors. They are usually formed in response to a life experience or a psychological trauma and can have both positive and negative effects on an individual's life.

Major Complexes in Jungian Psychology:

1. **The Father Complex:** This complex is related to the figure of the father or a fatherly authority. It can manifest in various ways, such as an excessive need for approval, a rebellion against authority, or an unconscious replication of the father's attitudes in one's life.

2. **The Mother Complex:** The mother complex is centered around the figure of the mother and can significantly influence an individual's relationships and emotional well-being. It may

result in dependency issues, challenges in forming relationships, or idealization or devaluation of maternal figures.

3. **The Shadow Complex:** The Shadow represents the repressed, dark, and often negative aspects of the personality. When not acknowledged, the Shadow complex can lead to destructive behavior patterns or projection of these unwanted qualities onto others.

4. **The Anima/Animus Complex:** This complex pertains to the unconscious feminine side in men (Anima) and the masculine side in women (Animus). Imbalances in this complex can affect relationships with the opposite sex and the integration of masculine and feminine aspects within oneself.

Impacts of Complexes:

- **Behavior and Personality:** Complexes can greatly influence a person's behavior, reactions, and personality traits. They can trigger emotional responses that are disproportionate to the situation, often leading to conflict or misunderstandings.

- **Psychological Development:** Complexes play a significant role in an individual's psychological development. Working through these complexes is often a part of the individuation process, leading to greater self-awareness and maturity.

- **Relationships:** Many complexes directly impact relationships. For example, unresolved father or mother complexes can influence how individuals relate to authority figures or partners.

- **Projection and Transference:** Complexes are often at the heart of projection and transference in relationships and therapy. Recognizing and understanding these dynamics is crucial in both personal development and in the therapeutic process.

Dealing with Complexes: The goal in Jungian psychology is not to eliminate complexes but to understand and integrate them. This involves bringing them into consciousness through therapy, self-reflection, and analysis, thereby reducing their unconscious control over behavior and emotions.

In essence, understanding and working through complexes is vital in Jungian therapy and personal growth. It's a process that leads to a more balanced, conscious, and integrated personality, allowing individuals to engage more healthily with themselves and the world around them.

7.3 Symbolism in Art and Culture

In Jungian psychology, the exploration of symbolism extends beyond the individual psyche into the realms of art and culture. Symbols in art and culture are seen as manifestations of the collective unconscious, reflecting shared human experiences, beliefs, and archetypes.

Symbolism in Art:

1. **Expression of the Unconscious:** Art serves as a conduit for expressing the unconscious. Artists often channel their internal experiences, including their dreams, fantasies, and unconscious conflicts, into their creations. This results in artworks that are rich in symbols and metaphors, revealing deeper psychological truths.

2. **Archetypal Themes:** Many artworks, whether in painting, literature, or film, depict archetypal themes and characters, such as the hero's journey, the mother figure, or the trickster. These archetypes resonate universally, tapping into shared human experiences and emotions.

3. **Therapeutic and Reflective Function:** Art can have a therapeutic effect, both on the creator and the viewer. Engaging with art allows for reflection, introspection, and a deeper understanding of oneself. It can also offer a form of catharsis, helping to process and integrate complex emotions and experiences.

Symbolism in Culture:

1. **Cultural Myths and Stories:** Myths, legends, and folklore are rich with symbolism and are considered expressions of the collective unconscious. They often contain universal truths and insights into the human condition, reflecting the fears, desires, and values of a culture.

2. **Rituals and Ceremonies:** Rituals and ceremonies, found in every culture, are steeped in symbolic actions and objects. They serve to connect individuals with collective values, traditions, and archetypal stories, playing a crucial role in societal bonding and personal transformation.

3. **Symbols as Cultural Connectors:** Symbols in culture act as connectors, linking individuals to their community, history, and shared human experience. They provide a sense of identity and belonging, and help in the transmission of cultural values and wisdom across generations.

The Universal Language of Symbols:

- **Commonality Across Cultures:** Despite cultural differences, certain symbols and themes appear universally in art and culture, suggesting a shared human psyche. For example, the concept of the Great Mother or the Wise Old Man appears in various forms across different cultures.

- **Interpretation and Diversity:** While some symbols are universal, their interpretation can vary greatly depending on cultural context. This diversity enriches the tapestry of human expression and understanding.

In conclusion, symbolism in art and culture plays a vital role in reflecting and shaping the human psyche. It not only provides insight into the collective unconscious but also serves as a bridge connecting individual experiences with universal human themes. Engaging with these symbols offers a deeper understanding of ourselves and our place in the world, transcending cultural and temporal boundaries.

7.4 Exercise: 10 MCQs with Answers at the End

1. In Jungian psychology, symbols in art and culture are seen as:

A. Random creative expressions

B. Manifestations of the collective unconscious

C. Direct representations of the artist's conscious thoughts

D. Irrelevant to understanding the human psyche

2. Which of the following is considered a universal archetype found in art and culture?

A. The specific historical event

B. The Trickster

C. A particular political ideology

D. A specific cultural practice

3. **The Father Complex in Jungian psychology often influences an individual's:**

A. Artistic preferences

B. Relationship with authority

C. Choice of career

D. Eating habits

4. **Artworks that feature common themes across various cultures are said to tap into:**

A. The artist's personal experience

B. The collective unconscious

C. Specific cultural values

D. Modern aesthetic trends

5. **Cultural myths and stories in Jungian psychology are viewed as:**

A. Purely entertainment

B. Historical accounts

C. Expressions of the collective unconscious

D. Outdated beliefs

6. **In Jungian therapy, integrating complexes is aimed at:**

A. Eliminating them entirely

B. Understanding and incorporating them into the psyche

C. Ignoring their influence

D. Focusing only on their negative aspects

7. **Rituals and ceremonies in different cultures are rich in:**

A. Financial expenditures

B. Symbolic actions and objects

C. Political statements

D. Scientific facts

8. **The therapeutic function of engaging with art in Jungian psychology involves:**

A. Increasing financial gain

B. Reflecting on and processing complex emotions

C. Gaining critical acclaim

D. Following societal trends

9. **The Anima/Animus complex in Jungian psychology refers to:**

A. The unconscious masculine side in women and feminine side in men

B. A preference for certain art forms

C. The dominant complex in all individuals

D. The fear of aging

10. Symbols in Jungian psychology are important because they:

A. Provide a precise literal interpretation of unconscious thoughts

B. Are aesthetically pleasing

C. Help in communicating deeper aspects of the psyche

D. Increase an individual's popularity

Answers

1. **B. Manifestations of the collective unconscious**

2. **B. The Trickster**

3. **B. Relationship with authority**

4. **B. The collective unconscious**

5. **C. Expressions of the collective unconscious**

6. **B. Understanding and incorporating them into the psyche**

7. **B. Symbolic actions and objects**

8. **B. Reflecting on and processing complex emotions**

9. **A. The unconscious masculine side in women and feminine side in men**

10. **C. Help in communicating deeper aspects of the psyche**

Chapter 8: Alchemy and Transformation

8.1 Historical Overview of Alchemy

Alchemy, often perceived as the medieval forerunner to modern chemistry, holds a much deeper and symbolic significance in the context of Jungian psychology. Its rich history and transformative symbolism provide a unique lens through which we can understand personal and psychological development.

The Origins of Alchemy: Alchemy's roots can be traced back to ancient civilizations, including Egypt and Greece, and it flourished in the Islamic and Western medieval worlds. Initially, it was a blend of practical experiments, mystical beliefs, and philosophical speculations, aimed at transmuting base metals into noble ones, particularly gold.

Spiritual and Philosophical Dimensions: Beyond its material goals, alchemy was imbued with spiritual and philosophical dimensions. Alchemists were not just seeking physical transformation but also spiritual enlightenment and the discovery of the universal elixir, believed to grant eternal life and ultimate wisdom.

Symbols in Alchemy: Alchemical processes are rich in symbolism. The transformation of base metals into gold was seen as a metaphor for spiritual purification and the attainment of higher states of consciousness. Symbols such as the philosopher's stone, the alchemical opus (the work), and various stages of the process (nigredo, albedo, rubedo) were laden with deep psychological meanings.

Jung's Interpretation of Alchemy: Carl Jung was deeply fascinated by alchemy and saw it as a symbolic representation of the process of individuation. He interpreted alchemical imagery as reflecting the unconscious processes involved in psychological development and transformation.

Alchemy as a Metaphor for Personal Growth: In Jungian psychology, the alchemical process is analogous to the psychological journey of transforming the self. The 'lead' represents the unrefined aspects of the personality, while the 'gold' symbolizes the achievement of wholeness and the realization of the true self.

Influence on Modern Psychology: Jung's exploration of alchemy had a significant impact on modern psychology, particularly in the field of depth psychology. He used alchemical symbolism to illustrate complex psychological concepts and to understand the transformative processes of the psyche.

In essence, the historical overview of alchemy reveals its profound impact on the psychological theories of Carl Jung. Alchemy, in this context, transcends its literal historical roots, serving as a rich metaphorical framework for understanding the profound and transformative journey of the human psyche.

8.2 Alchemical Symbols and Jungian Interpretation

Alchemy, with its enigmatic symbols and processes, plays a pivotal role in Jungian psychology. Carl Jung saw these symbols not as literal chemical processes but as metaphors for psychological transformation and growth. Let's explore some key alchemical symbols and their Jungian interpretations.

1. The Philosopher's Stone: In alchemy, the Philosopher's Stone is a legendary substance capable of turning base metals into gold and sometimes believed to grant immortality. Jung interpreted it as a symbol for the self, representing the final and most profound stage of individuation, where the conscious and unconscious are unified, and the individual reaches a state of wholeness.

2. Nigredo (Blackening): The first stage in the alchemical process is nigredo, associated with decay and disintegration. For Jung, this represented the initial stage of confronting the Shadow within the unconscious. It is a time of darkness and confusion, often marked by depression or a sense of despair, but it's a necessary phase for personal growth.

3. Albedo (Whitening): Following nigredo, albedo signifies purification and cleansing. Jung saw this as the process of becoming aware of and integrating the anima or animus, the opposite gender aspects within the psyche. It's a stage of self-reflection, insight, and often, revelations.

4. Rubedo (Reddening): The final stage, rubedo, symbolizes the achievement of wholeness and the integration of opposites. In Jungian terms, this is where true individuation occurs. The individual achieves a balance between the conscious and unconscious aspects of the psyche, symbolized by the marriage of the king and queen in alchemical texts.

5. The Ouroboros: Often depicted as a snake or dragon eating its own tail, the ouroboros is a symbol of the cyclical nature of alchemy, eternal return, and unity. Jung interpreted it as an indication of the self's cyclical nature of renewal and the eternal nature of the psyche.

6. The Coniunctio: This symbol represents the union of opposites, often depicted as the mystical marriage of the king and queen. In Jungian psychology, the coniunctio is analogous to the integration of the conscious and unconscious mind, resulting in the creation of the 'child,' a new state of being.

7. The Prima Materia: Often described as the starting material for the alchemical process, it is formless and holds the potential for transformation. Jung likened it to the original chaos or the unconscious from which the process of individuation begins.

In Jungian psychology, alchemical symbolism offers a rich and profound vocabulary for describing the transformative journey of the psyche. It provides a framework for understanding the depths and complexities of personal growth and the quest for psychological wholeness.

8.3 Psychological Alchemy and Personal Transformation

In Jungian psychology, psychological alchemy is more than a metaphor; it's a paradigm for understanding and facilitating personal transformation. This perspective views the process of psychological development as akin to the alchemical transmutation from base material into spiritual gold.

The Essence of Psychological Alchemy:

1. **Inner Transformation:** Psychological alchemy focuses on the transformation of the inner self. The goal is not the literal creation of gold but the metaphorical creation of a 'golden' personality – one that has achieved balance, wholeness, and integration of its disparate parts.

2. **Confronting the Shadow:** Just as alchemists begin with base materials, psychological alchemy often starts with confronting the Shadow – the unacknowledged, often negative, aspects of the self. This process involves recognizing and accepting these hidden parts, which is essential for personal growth.

3. **Integration of Opposites:** A core principle in psychological alchemy is the integration of opposites within the psyche, such as the conscious and unconscious, masculine and feminine, rational and irrational. This integration leads to the emergence of the Self, a central concept in Jungian psychology representing the unified whole.

Stages of Psychological Transformation:

1. **Nigredo – The Dark Night of the Soul:** This initial stage, characterized by disorientation and emotional turmoil, is where one becomes aware of the deeper, often darker, aspects of the psyche. It's a time of introspection and encountering the Shadow.

2. **Albedo – Purification and Insight:** After confronting the darkness, the individual moves into a phase of purification and clarification. This stage involves gaining insights into one's personality and behaviors and often includes exploring the anima or animus.

3. **Rubedo – The Reddening:** The final stage is where true individuation and integration occur. The individual achieves a balance between their various internal aspects, leading to a sense of wholeness and a newfound understanding of their place in the world.

Application in Therapy and Self-Development:

- Psychological alchemy provides a framework for therapy and self-development. It offers a structured approach to understanding one's psychological journey and the stages of personal growth.

- Therapists can use this model to help individuals navigate their inner transformations, providing guidance as they confront and integrate various aspects of their psyche.

The Transformative Power of Symbols and Dreams:

- In this process, symbols and dreams play a crucial role. They are seen as messages from the unconscious, providing insights and guidance on the journey towards wholeness.

Psychological alchemy in Jungian psychology is a profound and transformative journey. It encapsulates the essence of personal growth, mirroring the alchemical quest for transformation and enlightenment. This journey is not just about resolving psychological issues but about realizing the full potential of the Self.

8.4 Exercise: 10 MCQs with Answers at the End

1. **In Jungian psychology, psychological alchemy primarily symbolizes:**

   A. The process of turning base metals into gold

   B. The literal creation of the philosopher's stone

C. Personal and psychological transformation

D. Historical chemical practices

2. The first stage in psychological alchemy, 'Nigredo,' represents:

A. Emotional stability and happiness

B. Confrontation with the Shadow and inner turmoil

C. The final stage of personal development

D. The discovery of one's true desires

3. In the context of psychological alchemy, what does the 'Philosopher's Stone' symbolize?

A. A real stone with magical properties

B. The attainment of material wealth

C. The unification and wholeness of the self

D. A tool used by medieval alchemists

4. The stage of 'Albedo' in psychological alchemy is associated with:

A. Purification and gaining insights

B. Ignoring personal flaws

C. External changes in one's life

D. Achieving career goals

5. **'Rubedo,' the final stage in psychological alchemy, signifies:**

A. The beginning of the alchemical process

B. A return to the Nigredo stage

C. The achievement of balance and wholeness

D. Physical rejuvenation

6. **In Jungian psychology, confronting and integrating the Shadow involves:**

A. Rejecting negative aspects of the self

B. Acknowledging and accepting repressed parts of the psyche

C. Focusing only on positive personal traits

D. Changing one's personality completely

7. **The integration of opposites in the psyche during psychological alchemy can lead to:**

A. Increased internal conflict

B. The emergence of the Self

C. Loss of personal identity

D. A preference for solitude

8. **The role of symbols and dreams in psychological alchemy is to:**

A. Predict the future

B. Provide entertainment

C. Offer insights and guidance from the unconscious

D. Recall past life experiences

9. **Psychological alchemy in therapy helps individuals:**

A. Gain material success

B. Navigate their inner transformations

C. Learn historical facts about alchemy

D. Improve their physical health

10. **The overall goal of psychological alchemy in Jungian psychology is:**

A. To perfect chemical processes

B. To attain external validation

C. Personal growth and realization of the Self

D. To eliminate all personal flaws

Answers

1. **C. Personal and psychological transformation**

2. **B. Confrontation with the Shadow and inner turmoil**

3. **C. The unification and wholeness of the self**

4. **A. Purification and gaining insights**

5. **C. The achievement of balance and wholeness**

6. **B. Acknowledging and accepting repressed parts of the psyche**

7. **B. The emergence of the Self**

8. **C. Offer insights and guidance from the unconscious**

9. **B. Navigate their inner transformations**

10. **C. Personal growth and realization of the Self**

Chapter 9: Jung's Influence on Modern Therapy

9.1 Jungian Analysis: Principles and Techniques

Jungian analysis, or analytical psychology, has had a profound impact on modern therapy. This therapeutic approach, developed by Carl Jung, is distinctive for its depth and focus on the integration of the conscious and unconscious parts of the psyche. Let's delve into the core principles and techniques of Jungian analysis.

Core Principles of Jungian Analysis:

1. **Individuation:** The primary goal of Jungian analysis is the process of individuation, which involves realizing and integrating the different aspects of the self. This process leads to greater self-awareness and psychological wholeness.

2. **The Role of the Unconscious:** Jungian therapy places significant emphasis on exploring the unconscious mind, including dreams, fantasies, and symbols. It acknowledges the profound influence of the unconscious on behavior and emotions.

3. **Integration of Opposites:** Jung believed in the importance of balancing opposing forces within the psyche, such as the conscious and unconscious, masculinity and femininity, rationality and irrationality. This integration is crucial for achieving psychological health.

Key Techniques in Jungian Analysis:

1. **Dream Analysis:** Dreams are viewed as direct communications from the unconscious and are analyzed for their symbolic content and meaning. This technique helps uncover repressed aspects of the psyche and provides insight into the individuation process.

2. **Active Imagination:** This involves engaging with the contents of the unconscious in a meditative state. The client actively participates in the exploration of fantasies, images, and internal narratives, facilitating a dialogue between the conscious and unconscious mind.

3. **Exploration of Complexes:** Jungian therapists work with clients to identify and explore complexes – emotional patterns and beliefs that have a powerful influence on an individual's behavior and psychological state.

4. **Use of Symbolism:** Jungian analysis often involves interpreting the symbolism in art, dreams, and fantasies. This helps in accessing and understanding deeper psychological truths.

5. **Transference and Countertransference:** The dynamics of transference (the client's projection of unconscious feelings onto the therapist) and countertransference (the therapist's reactions to the client) are considered crucial in the therapeutic process and are used to gain insight into the client's psyche.

6. **Myth and Narrative:** Stories, myths, and narratives are used in therapy as mirrors to understand and explain life patterns and psychological issues. They provide a rich source of symbolism and archetypal themes relevant to the client's experience.

Jungian analysis is a deeply introspective and transformative approach to therapy. It extends beyond symptom relief, offering a path to self-discovery and personal growth. This form of therapy is particularly effective for individuals seeking to explore the deeper aspects of their personality and resolve complex emotional and psychological issues.

9.2 Applications in Various Therapeutic Settings

Jungian analysis, with its deep exploration of the unconscious, has wide-ranging applications in various therapeutic settings. Its principles can be adapted to address a variety of psychological issues and are employed in different contexts to facilitate healing and personal growth.

1. Individual Therapy:

- **Personal Growth and Self-Discovery:** Jungian therapy is particularly effective for clients seeking a deeper understanding of themselves. It's used to explore personal narratives, dreams, and unconscious patterns that influence behavior and relationships.

- **Dealing with Depression and Anxiety:** By exploring the underlying unconscious factors contributing to these conditions, Jungian therapy can provide insights and coping strategies.

2. Group Therapy:

- **Exploring Collective Dynamics:** In group settings, Jungian principles can help explore collective unconscious dynamics and shared archetypal themes. This approach can foster a deeper understanding of group behavior and interpersonal relationships.

3. Family Therapy:

- **Addressing Family Dynamics:** Jungian therapy can be used to explore family dynamics and unconscious patterns passed down through generations. It helps family members understand each other's psychological makeup and improves communication.

4. Couples Therapy:

- **Relationship Dynamics:** Jungian analysis is helpful in couples therapy for exploring the dynamics of the anima and animus within the relationship. It aids in understanding how unconscious projections and expectations affect the relationship.

5. Art and Creative Therapy:

- **Expression Through Art:** Jungian therapy integrates well with art and creative therapies, providing a means for clients to express and explore unconscious material through artistic mediums.

6. Trauma and Grief Counseling:

- **Processing Traumatic Experiences:** The exploration of the unconscious in Jungian therapy can be crucial in helping individuals process and integrate traumatic experiences or grief.

7. Career Counseling:

- **Aligning with Personal Goals:** Jungian principles can guide individuals in understanding their deeper aspirations and choosing career paths aligned with their true selves.

8. Dream Workshops and Retreats:

- **Focus on Dream Interpretation:** Jungian analysis is often a central component of workshops and retreats focusing on dream interpretation, helping participants gain insights into their unconscious mind.

9. Adolescence and Youth Counseling:

- **Identity Formation:** Jungian therapy can aid adolescents in navigating the challenges of identity formation and self-discovery during crucial developmental stages.

10. Spiritual Counseling:

- **Exploring Spirituality:** Jungian therapy often delves into the spiritual dimension of the psyche, making it suitable for individuals seeking to explore and integrate spiritual experiences.

The versatility of Jungian analysis in various therapeutic settings lies in its emphasis on understanding the whole person – conscious and unconscious – and its recognition of the deep psychological undercurrents that shape human behavior and experience. This approach facilitates not just symptom relief but a journey towards greater self-awareness and fulfillment.

9.3 Integrating Jungian Concepts in Modern Therapy

The integration of Jungian concepts into modern therapy has enriched the practice of psychotherapy, offering unique perspectives and tools for understanding and facilitating psychological growth. Jung's ideas have been blended with various therapeutic modalities, expanding the ways in which therapists can address the needs of their clients.

1. Depth Psychology:

- Jung's concepts form the cornerstone of depth psychology, a field that emphasizes the exploration of the unconscious. Techniques like dream analysis and active imagination are commonly used to delve into the deeper layers of the psyche.

2. Cognitive Behavioral Therapy (CBT):

- While CBT is primarily focused on conscious thought processes and behaviors, integrating Jungian concepts can enhance its effectiveness by addressing the underlying unconscious patterns that contribute to cognitive and behavioral issues.

3. Humanistic and Existential Therapies:

- Jung's emphasis on individuation and self-realization aligns well with the goals of humanistic and existential therapies. These modalities often incorporate Jungian concepts to explore clients' search for meaning, identity, and self-actualization.

4. Psychodynamic Therapy:

- Many Jungian principles, particularly those related to the exploration of the unconscious and early life experiences, are integrated into psychodynamic therapy, enriching its understanding of personal history and its impact on current behavior.

5. Art Therapy:

- Jung's appreciation of symbolism and the creative process finds a natural application in art therapy. Clients are encouraged to express their unconscious through art, facilitating healing and self-discovery.

6. Family Systems Therapy:

- Jungian concepts, especially those concerning archetypes and family dynamics, are applied in family systems therapy to understand family roles and intergenerational patterns.

7. Trauma-Informed Approaches:

- Jungian perspectives on the shadow and personal transformation can be particularly valuable in trauma-informed therapy, helping clients integrate and heal from traumatic experiences.

8. Mindfulness and Body-Centered Therapies:

- Integrating Jungian concepts with mindfulness and body-centered therapies can enhance self-awareness and the understanding of the mind-body connection.

9. Eclectic and Integrative Approaches:

- Many modern therapists adopt an eclectic approach, combining Jungian methods with other therapeutic techniques to create personalized treatment plans that address the unique needs of each client.

10. Online and Teletherapy Platforms:

- Jungian concepts are also being adapted for online and teletherapy formats, making them accessible to a wider audience and fitting them into contemporary lifestyles.

The integration of Jungian concepts into modern therapy has broadened the scope of therapeutic practice, offering a holistic approach that acknowledges the complexity of the human psyche. By blending Jung's insights with other therapeutic techniques, practitioners can address a wide range of psychological issues with greater depth and efficacy.

9.4 Exercise: 10 MCQs with Answers at the End

1. **Jungian psychology is foundational to which field of therapy?**

    A. Cognitive Behavioral Therapy

    B. Depth Psychology

    C. Solution-Focused Brief Therapy

    D. Behaviorism

2. **In modern therapy, Jung's concept of the Shadow is often explored in:**

   A. Positive Psychology

   B. Trauma-Informed Approaches

   C. Behavior Modification Techniques

   D. Systematic Desensitization

3. **Active Imagination, a technique developed by Jung, is used in therapy to:**

   A. Control unwanted behaviors

   B. Facilitate a dialogue between conscious and unconscious mind

   C. Improve memory recall

   D. Increase focus and concentration

4. **Jungian concepts have been integrated into Cognitive Behavioral Therapy to:**

   A. Address underlying unconscious patterns

   B. Focus solely on behavioral change

   C. Avoid exploring past experiences

   D. Enhance physical well-being

5. In family systems therapy, Jungian concepts help understand:

A. Genetic influences on behavior

B. Family roles and intergenerational patterns

C. Financial management within families

D. Legal aspects of family disputes

6. Which therapy aligns with Jung's emphasis on individuation and self-realization?

A. Humanistic and Existential Therapies

B. Rational Emotive Behavior Therapy

C. Dialectical Behavior Therapy

D. Exposure Therapy

7. Jung's appreciation of symbolism finds application in:

A. Art Therapy

B. Occupational Therapy

C. Speech Therapy

D. Physical Therapy

8. **Jungian psychology in trauma-informed therapy helps clients:**

   A. Avoid confronting traumatic experiences

   B. Integrate and heal from traumatic experiences

   C. Focus only on present issues

   D. Disregard past experiences

9. **Eclectic and integrative approaches in therapy:**

   A. Exclude Jungian methods

   B. Combine Jungian methods with other therapeutic techniques

   C. Focus only on Jungian analysis

   D. Are based solely on cognitive theories

10. **Jungian concepts in mindfulness and body-centered therapies enhance:**

   A. Athletic performance

   B. Self-awareness and understanding of the mind-body connection

   C. Mathematical skills

   D. Technical skills in computer programming

Answers

1. **B. Depth Psychology**

2. **B. Trauma-Informed Approaches**

3. **B. Facilitate a dialogue between conscious and unconscious mind**

4. **A. Address underlying unconscious patterns**

5. **B. Family roles and intergenerational patterns**

6. **A. Humanistic and Existential Therapies**

7. **A. Art Therapy**

8. **B. Integrate and heal from traumatic experiences**

9. **B. Combine Jungian methods with other therapeutic techniques**

10. **B. Self-awareness and understanding of the mind-body connection**

Chapter 10: Religion and Spirituality

10.1 Jung's Views on Religion

Carl Jung's views on religion were complex and nuanced, reflecting his deep engagement with the psychological significance of religious and spiritual experiences. He saw religion not just as a societal institution but as a profound expression of the human psyche's search for meaning.

Religion as a Manifestation of the Psyche:

1. **Symbolic Understanding:** Jung viewed religious symbols and narratives as expressions of the collective unconscious. He believed that religious symbols and rituals played a crucial role in representing and communicating the deeper aspects of the human psyche.

2. **Psychological Function of Religion:** For Jung, religion served an essential psychological function. It provided a framework for individuals to explore and relate to the transcendent aspects of human experience, offering a means of psychological orientation and stability.

3. **Personal and Collective Experience:** Jung differentiated between personal religious experience and institutional religion. He was more interested in personal, individual experiences of the numinous (a profound spiritual or mystical experience) than in dogma or religious institutions.

Integration of Religion and Psychology:

1. **Religion in Individual Development:** Jung believed that religious experiences could play a vital role in individual development, particularly in the process of individuation. He saw the exploration of religious and spiritual experiences as integral to understanding the self.

2. **Critique of Modern Religion:** Jung critiqued modern religions for often failing to connect with the deeper, symbolic aspects of the psyche. He believed that for religion to be psychologically beneficial, it needed to resonate with the individual's inner experiences.

3. **The Role of Myths and Symbols:** Jung placed significant importance on religious myths and symbols, seeing them as expressions of archetypal truths. He suggested that myths and religious narratives provide a language for discussing and understanding the otherwise inexpressible aspects of human experience.

The Universality of Religious Themes:

1. **Archetypal Themes in Religion:** Jung explored various religions and found common archetypal themes, such as the

hero's journey, death and rebirth, and the mother archetype. He argued that these themes reflected universal aspects of the human experience.

2. **Religion and the Unconscious:** Jung believed that religions across the world emerged from the collective unconscious, embodying the shared experiences and psychic realities of humanity.

In summary, Jung's approach to religion was deeply psychological. He valued religious and spiritual experiences for their power to express and explore the depths of the human psyche, and he saw them as essential to the process of achieving personal wholeness and understanding the collective human experience. His work offers a bridge between the realms of psychology and spirituality, emphasizing the importance of both in understanding the human condition.

10.2 Symbolism and Religious Experiences

Carl Jung's exploration of symbolism and religious experiences unveils a profound intersection between psychology and spirituality. Jung viewed religious symbols and experiences not just as elements of faith traditions but as essential expressions of deep psychological truths.

Understanding Symbolism in Religion:

1. **Symbols as Bridges:** Jung saw religious symbols as bridges between the conscious and the unconscious mind, conveying truths that transcend rational understanding. These symbols often encapsulate complex spiritual and psychological realities in a way that words cannot.

2. **Universal Archetypes:** Many religious symbols correspond to universal archetypes found in the collective unconscious. For example, the figure of the Great Mother in various religions is an expression of the mother archetype, representing creation, fertility, and nurturing.

3. **Personal and Collective Significance:** Religious symbols can have both a personal and collective significance. They resonate with the personal psyche, reflecting individual spiritual experiences, while also connecting individuals to the wider human experience.

Experiencing the Numinous:

1. **The Concept of the Numinous:** Jung adopted Rudolf Otto's concept of the numinous to describe the experience of encountering a presence or reality that is wholly other, evoking a mixed reaction of fear and fascination. Such experiences are central in many religions.

2. **Religious Experiences as Encounters with the Unconscious:** Jung viewed religious experiences, such as mystical visions or profound spiritual insights, as encounters with the deeper

aspects of the unconscious. These experiences often bring about a significant psychological transformation.

Impact of Religious Experiences:

1. **Transformation and Individuation:** Religious experiences can be transformative, facilitating the process of individuation, or the integration and harmonization of the self. They can lead to a deeper understanding of oneself and one's place in the world.

2. **Healing and Wholeness:** Jung believed that religious experiences and symbols could have a healing effect on the psyche, providing a sense of meaning, purpose, and connection that contributes to overall psychological well-being.

3. **Confrontation with the Shadow:** Religious experiences often involve confronting the Shadow, or the darker aspects of the psyche, as part of spiritual growth and self-realization.

Jung's Inclusive Approach to Religion:

1. **Interfaith Perspective:** Jung was interested in a wide range of religious traditions, seeing value in diverse religious symbols and practices. He believed that understanding these various expressions of spirituality could enrich psychological understanding.

2. **Critique of Literalism:** Jung cautioned against the literal interpretation of religious symbols, arguing that such an

approach misses the deeper, symbolic meanings that are vital for psychological insight and growth.

In Jung's perspective, the exploration of symbolism and religious experiences is crucial in understanding the human psyche. These elements provide a rich tapestry of insights into the spiritual dimension of human life, reflecting the universal quest for meaning and connection.

10.3 The Spiritual Dimension in Psychological Health

Carl Jung's approach to psychology significantly recognized the importance of the spiritual dimension in overall psychological health. He believed that spirituality is a fundamental aspect of the human experience and plays a crucial role in an individual's mental and emotional well-being.

Integration of Spirituality in Psychological Well-Being:

1. **Spirituality as a Source of Meaning:** Jung saw spirituality as a key source of meaning and purpose in life. He believed that a lack of spiritual connection could lead to a sense of emptiness and disconnection, often manifesting in symptoms of psychological distress.

2. **Individuation and Spiritual Growth:** The process of individuation, central to Jung's theory, involves the integration

of various aspects of the psyche, including the spiritual. Personal spiritual beliefs and experiences are seen as essential components of self-discovery and self-realization.

The Role of Religious and Spiritual Symbols:

1. **Symbols as Mediators:** Religious and spiritual symbols serve as mediators between the conscious and unconscious mind. They help individuals connect with and express deep psychological and spiritual truths.

2. **Archetypal Dimensions of Spirituality:** Jung emphasized the archetypal nature of religious symbols and rituals, viewing them as expressions of universal human experiences. This perspective allows for a psychological understanding of religious phenomena across different cultures.

Spirituality in Coping and Resilience:

1. **Coping with Life Transitions and Losses:** Spirituality often provides a framework for coping with life transitions, losses, and traumas. It offers a sense of continuity and a context for understanding and integrating these experiences.

2. **Building Resilience:** A strong spiritual orientation can contribute to psychological resilience, offering resources for dealing with stress, adversity, and the challenges of life.

Jung's Inclusive View of Spirituality:

1. **Beyond Organized Religion:** Jung's understanding of spirituality extended beyond organized religion. He valued personal spiritual experiences and the exploration of diverse religious traditions as pathways to psychological depth and wholeness.

2. **Spirituality and the Unconscious:** Jung viewed spirituality as deeply connected to the unconscious. He believed that engaging with the spiritual dimension could bring unconscious contents into consciousness, facilitating psychological healing and growth.

Therapeutic Implications:

1. **Holistic Approach to Therapy:** Jungian therapy often incorporates the individual's spiritual beliefs and experiences as an integral part of the therapeutic process.

2. **Addressing Spiritual Crises:** Jungian therapists may work with clients experiencing spiritual crises, helping them to explore and integrate these experiences into their psychological understanding.

In summary, Jung's approach highlights the interconnection between spirituality and psychological health. He advocates for an inclusive and holistic view of the human psyche, where spiritual beliefs and experiences are recognized as vital components in achieving psychological balance and well-being.

10.4 Exercise: 10 MCQs with Answers at the End

1. **According to Jung, spirituality in psychology primarily serves as:**

   A. A means of avoiding reality

   B. A source of meaning and purpose

   C. A way to adhere to societal norms

   D. A method for achieving financial success

2. **Jung's concept of individuation includes the integration of:**

   A. Only the conscious mind

   B. Spiritual and psychological aspects

   C. Physical health above mental health

   D. Social status and wealth

3. **In Jungian psychology, religious and spiritual symbols are viewed as:**

   A. Literal historical accounts

   B. Mediators between the conscious and unconscious mind

   C. Irrelevant to modern life

   D. Only applicable within specific religious contexts

4. **Spiritual experiences in Jungian therapy are often explored for their:**

   A. Entertainment value

   B. Connection to unconscious processes

   C. Impact on physical health

   D. Influence on technological advancement

5. **Jung's approach to spirituality is characterized by:**

   A. Strict adherence to a single religious doctrine

   B. An inclusive exploration of diverse religious traditions

   C. Dismissal of all organized religions

   D. Focus on external religious practices

6. **Spirituality can contribute to psychological resilience by:**

   A. Promoting material wealth

   B. Providing resources for dealing with stress and adversity

   C. Encouraging competition

   D. Enhancing technological skills

7. **In Jungian therapy, addressing spiritual crises involves:**

   A. Ignoring spiritual experiences

   B. Exploring and integrating these experiences

   C. Focusing solely on medical interventions

D. Promoting a specific religious belief

8. Jung believed that a lack of spiritual connection could lead to:

A. Increased physical strength

B. A sense of emptiness and disconnection

C. Improved rational thinking

D. Enhanced artistic abilities

9. Jung viewed religious myths and symbols as expressions of:

A. Outdated beliefs

B. Universal human experiences

C. Specific cultural practices

D. Individual artistic talent

10. The role of archetypal dimensions in spirituality, according to Jung, is to:

A. Create rigid dogmas

B. Express universal human experiences

C. Promote specific political ideologies

D. Focus on technological development

Answers

1. **B. A source of meaning and purpose**

2. **B. Spiritual and psychological aspects**

3. **B. Mediators between the conscious and unconscious mind**

4. **B. Connection to unconscious processes**

5. **B. An inclusive exploration of diverse religious traditions**

6. **B. Providing resources for dealing with stress and adversity**

7. **B. Exploring and integrating these experiences**

8. **B. A sense of emptiness and disconnection**

9. **B. Universal human experiences**

10. **B. Express universal human experiences**

Chapter 11: Art, Creativity, and the Psyche

11.1 The Creative Process in Jungian Psychology

In Jungian psychology, the creative process is viewed not just as a means of artistic expression but as a fundamental component of psychological development and self-expression. Carl Jung saw creativity as a bridge between the conscious and the unconscious mind, a pathway to individuation and personal growth.

Understanding the Creative Process:

1. **Expression of the Unconscious:** Jung believed that creativity is an expression of the unconscious, bringing to light the unseen, unacknowledged, and often unarticulated aspects of the psyche. Artistic creation can therefore be a form of dialogue with the unconscious.

2. **Creativity as a Healing Process:** Engaging in creative activities can have a therapeutic effect, helping to resolve internal conflicts, explore emotions, and express feelings that might be difficult to verbalize. The act of creating can be a cathartic experience, providing relief and insight.

3. **Symbolism in Creativity:** Much like in dreams, symbols play a crucial role in the creative process. Art often utilizes symbolic imagery to convey deeper meanings and explore complex psychological themes.

The Role of Archetypes in Creativity:

1. **Archetypal Themes:** Creative works frequently embody archetypal themes and characters, reflecting the universal human experiences that reside in the collective unconscious. These can range from the hero's journey to the exploration of the shadow self.

2. **Personal and Collective Resonance:** Art has the ability to resonate on both a personal and a collective level, tapping into shared human emotions and experiences. This dual resonance can make artistic expression profoundly impactful.

Creative Individuation:

1. **Self-Discovery and Development:** The creative process is a means of self-discovery and development. It can facilitate the individuation process, as it often involves exploring and integrating various aspects of the self.

2. **Transformation Through Creativity:** Engaging in creative endeavors can lead to personal transformation. As individuals express and reconcile different parts of their psyche through art, they can experience growth, insight, and a sense of wholeness.

Creativity in Therapy:

1. **Art Therapy:** In Jungian therapy, art can be used as a tool for exploration and healing. Clients may be encouraged to engage in artistic activities to access and work through unconscious material.

2. **Interpreting Artistic Expressions:** Therapists may work with clients to interpret their artworks, exploring the symbolism and emotions they contain to gain insight into the clients' psychological states and processes.

In summary, the creative process in Jungian psychology is deeply intertwined with the dynamics of the psyche. It is a means of exploring the unconscious, expressing the inexpressible, and facilitating psychological growth and healing. The act of creating becomes more than an artistic endeavor; it becomes a journey into the depths of the self.

11.2 Analyzing Art through a Jungian Lens

Analyzing art through a Jungian lens involves delving into the deeper symbolic meanings and psychological dimensions that artworks may embody. Carl Jung's insights into the unconscious, archetypes, and symbolic language provide a rich framework for interpreting art, offering a window into both the collective human experience and individual psyche.

Key Aspects of Jungian Art Analysis:

1. **Symbolic Interpretation:** Jungian analysis of art focuses on decoding the symbolic language used in artworks. Symbols in art are seen as expressions of the unconscious, conveying meanings and emotions that go beyond the literal or obvious.

2. **Archetypal Themes:** Artworks are often explored for their archetypal content. Jungian analysts look for universal themes and characters, such as the hero, the mother, the trickster, or the shadow, which resonate with the collective unconscious.

3. **Personal Unconscious and Individuation:** Art is also seen as a manifestation of the artist's personal unconscious. It can reflect the artist's inner conflicts, desires, fears, and journey towards individuation. Analyzing art can reveal how artists negotiate their personal growth and self-understanding.

4. **Cultural and Historical Context:** While interpreting art, Jungian analysts also consider the cultural and historical context of the artwork. This includes exploring how the collective unconscious of a particular time or culture may have influenced the artist and their work.

5. **Emotional and Psychological Impact:** The emotional and psychological impact of an artwork on viewers is another key aspect. Art can evoke deep emotional responses and insights, offering viewers a means of connecting with their own unconscious material.

The Process of Analyzing Art in Jungian Terms:

1. **Identifying Symbols:** The first step is identifying the symbols present in the artwork and exploring their possible meanings, both universal and personal.

2. **Exploring Archetypes:** Analysts consider which archetypes are represented in the artwork and how these archetypes relate to universal human experiences and psychological processes.

3. **Personal Resonance:** The personal resonance and emotional reactions of both the artist and the viewer to the artwork are explored to understand how it reflects individual psychological states.

4. **Contextual Analysis:** The cultural, historical, and personal background of the artist is considered to provide a deeper understanding of the artwork's themes and symbolism.

5. **Integration and Insight:** The final goal is to integrate the insights gained from the analysis, understanding how the artwork contributes to our knowledge of human psychology and individual self-awareness.

In summary, analyzing art through a Jungian lens is a multi-layered process that goes beyond aesthetic appreciation. It involves a deep exploration of the symbolic and archetypal content, revealing the profound psychological insights that art can offer into the human condition and individual psyche.

11.3 The Role of Creativity in Self-Realization

In Jungian psychology, creativity is not just an artistic endeavor but a vital component of self-realization and personal development. Carl Jung perceived creativity as a process that extends beyond the production of art, encompassing a broader spectrum of self-expression and exploration.

Creativity as a Path to the Unconscious:

1. **Expression of the Inner Self:** Creativity allows for the expression of the inner self, including aspects of the unconscious mind. It provides a means to articulate feelings, thoughts, and experiences that might be difficult to express in words.

2. **Dialogue with the Unconscious:** Engaging in creative activities is seen as a form of dialogue with the unconscious. It can reveal hidden desires, fears, and aspects of the personality, facilitating a deeper understanding of oneself.

Creativity and Individuation:

1. **Facilitating Individuation:** Creativity is closely linked to the process of individuation – the development of an integrated self. Through creative expression, individuals can explore and reconcile different parts of their psyche, leading to greater wholeness and self-awareness.

2. **Integration of the Persona and Shadow:** Creative activities can help integrate the persona (the social self) and the shadow (the repressed aspects of the personality). This integration is crucial for achieving authenticity and self-realization.

Creative Expression and Personal Growth:

1. **Developing Potential:** Creativity is a means of developing and realizing personal potential. It allows individuals to explore their capabilities and interests, pushing the boundaries of their self-concept.

2. **Transformative Power of Creativity:** The act of creating can be transformative. It often leads to personal insights, emotional catharsis, and a sense of accomplishment and fulfillment.

Therapeutic Benefits of Creativity:

1. **Healing through Art:** In therapy, creative expression is used as a tool for healing. It can help process emotions, manage stress, and work through trauma.

2. **Enhancing Mental Health:** Regular engagement in creative activities has been linked to improved mental health, including reduced anxiety and depression, and increased feelings of well-being.

Broadening the Definition of Creativity:

1. **Beyond Artistic Expression:** Jung's concept of creativity extends beyond traditional artistic expression. It includes any form of innovative thinking, problem-solving, and personal expression that contributes to the individual's development.

2. **Creativity in Everyday Life:** Creativity can be expressed in everyday life, in how individuals approach tasks, solve problems, and engage with the world around them.

In Jungian psychology, creativity is a key vehicle for self-discovery and self-realization. It's a process that allows individuals to connect with their innermost selves, explore their potential, and achieve a more integrated and authentic sense of self.

11.4 Exercise: 10 MCQs with Answers at the End

1. **In Jungian psychology, creativity is primarily viewed as:**

   A. A means for artistic expression only

B. A tool for professional advancement

C. A path to self-realization and exploring the unconscious

D. Irrelevant to personal development

2. Which aspect of the psyche is directly engaged through creative activities according to Jung?

A. The conscious mind only

B. The ego

C. The unconscious mind

D. The persona

3. The process of individuation in Jungian psychology involves:

A. Avoiding any creative activities

B. Developing and integrating various aspects of the self

C. Focusing solely on intellectual pursuits

D. Conforming to societal norms

4. Creativity in Jungian therapy can help in:

A. Suppressing unwanted emotions

B. Processing emotions and managing stress

C. Increasing financial success

D. Enhancing only artistic skills

5. **Regular engagement in creative activities is linked to:**

   A. Decreased cognitive abilities

   B. Improved mental health and well-being

   C. Reduced physical health

   D. Limited personal expression

6. **In Jungian psychology, the integration of the persona and the shadow through creativity leads to:**

   A. Loss of identity

   B. Greater authenticity and self-awareness

   C. A heightened sense of ego

   D. Decreased self-esteem

7. **Jung's concept of creativity extends beyond:**

   A. Traditional artistic expression

   B. Basic cognitive functions

   C. Physical activities

   D. Technological innovations

8. **The transformative power of creativity in Jungian psychology is associated with:**

   A. Personal insights and emotional catharsis

   B. External recognition and fame

C. Mastery of specific art forms

D. Achieving financial independence

9. **Creativity in everyday life, according to Jung, involves:**

A. Strict adherence to routines

B. Innovative thinking and problem-solving

C. Avoiding new experiences

D. Focusing only on practical tasks

10. **The role of creativity in Jungian therapy includes:**

A. Discouraging personal expression

B. Healing and exploring deeper aspects of the psyche

C. Promoting a singular focus on artistic skills

D. Ignoring the unconscious processes

Answers

1. **C. A path to self-realization and exploring the unconscious**

2. **C. The unconscious mind**

3. **B. Developing and integrating various aspects of the self**

4. **B.** Processing emotions and managing stress

5. **B.** Improved mental health and well-being

6. **B.** Greater authenticity and self-awareness

7. **A.** Traditional artistic expression

8. **A.** Personal insights and emotional catharsis

9. **B.** Innovative thinking and problem-solving

10. **B.** Healing and exploring deeper aspects of the psyche

Chapter 12: The Shadow and the Self

12.1 Exploring the Shadow

In Jungian psychology, the concept of the Shadow holds a significant place. It represents the unconscious aspect of the personality which the conscious ego does not recognize in itself. Understanding and integrating the Shadow is crucial for personal growth and self-awareness.

Understanding the Shadow:

1. **The Unconscious Aspect:** The Shadow is composed of repressed ideas, weaknesses, desires, instincts, and shortcomings. It encompasses all that the individual does not consciously acknowledge or accept.

2. **Projection of the Shadow:** Often, individuals project their Shadow onto others, seeing their own undesirable traits in them. This projection can lead to misunderstandings and conflicts in relationships.

3. **Role in Personal Development:** Confronting and integrating the Shadow is essential for individuation. Acknowledging and

accepting the Shadow leads to a more complete and balanced self.

Exploring the Shadow:

1. **Recognition and Acceptance:** The first step in exploring the Shadow is recognizing that it exists. This involves a willingness to look at parts of oneself that might be uncomfortable or socially unacceptable.

2. **Reflection and Self-Examination:** Through introspection, individuals can identify aspects of their Shadow. This might involve reflecting on emotional reactions, dreams, or fantasies.

3. **Therapeutic Exploration:** In therapy, techniques like dream analysis, active imagination, and dialogue can help uncover and understand the Shadow.

4. **Transformation Through Integration:** Integrating the Shadow does not mean acting out on these repressed aspects but rather acknowledging them as part of the whole self. This integration can lead to significant personal transformation.

Challenges in Shadow Work:

1. **Emotional Difficulty:** Exploring the Shadow can be emotionally challenging, as it involves facing parts of oneself that may cause shame, guilt, or fear.

2. **Resistance:** There is often a natural resistance to confronting the Shadow, as it challenges the ego's perception of itself.

3. **Continuous Process:** Shadow work is not a one-time event but an ongoing process in personal development.

Benefits of Shadow Work:

1. **Increased Self-Awareness:** Understanding the Shadow leads to greater self-awareness and authenticity.

2. **Improved Relationships:** By recognizing one's own projections, individuals can improve their relationships and interactions with others.

3. **Psychological Growth:** Integrating the Shadow is crucial for psychological growth and achieving a sense of wholeness.

Exploring the Shadow in Jungian psychology is a journey towards acknowledging and integrating the hidden aspects of the self. It is a vital step towards achieving a balanced personality and a deeper understanding of oneself and one's interactions with the world.

12.2 The Journey towards Wholeness and Integration

In Jungian psychology, the journey towards wholeness and integration is a central theme, often referred to as the process of individuation. This journey involves acknowledging and integrating various aspects of the psyche, including the conscious and unconscious, the ego, the shadow, and the anima/animus, to achieve a balanced and holistic self.

Understanding the Journey:

1. **Individuation:** This is the process of becoming aware of oneself as a distinct and whole individual. It involves differentiating oneself from societal norms and expectations and integrating various aspects of the psyche.

2. **Integration of the Conscious and Unconscious:** A key aspect of this journey is the integration of the conscious mind with the contents of the unconscious, including the shadow. This involves acknowledging and processing unconscious material, which can include repressed memories, desires, and aspects of the self.

Stages of the Journey:

1. **Confrontation with the Shadow:** This stage involves facing the darker aspects of the personality, the traits and impulses that are rejected by the conscious self.

2. **Encounter with Anima/Animus:** Here, one confronts the anima or animus, which represents the feminine aspects in males and the masculine aspects in females. This encounter helps to balance gender-related aspects within the psyche.

3. **Realization of the Persona:** Understanding and differentiating the persona (the social mask) from the true self is another important step. It involves recognizing and shedding the roles played to conform to societal expectations.

4. **Integration and Self-Realization:** The final stage is the integration of these disparate parts into a cohesive whole, leading to self-realization and the development of a unique individual identity.

Challenges on the Path:

1. **Emotional and Psychological Resistance:** The journey is often fraught with resistance as confronting the shadow and other unconscious elements can be unsettling and emotionally challenging.

2. **Transformational Crisis:** Individuals may go through periods of crisis during this process, which are necessary for growth and transformation.

Benefits of the Journey:

1. **Greater Self-Awareness:** This journey leads to increased self-awareness and understanding of one's motivations, desires, and fears.

2. **Enhanced Relationships:** By understanding oneself better, individuals can form healthier and more authentic relationships.

3. **Personal Growth and Fulfillment:** Achieving a sense of wholeness leads to personal fulfillment and a more meaningful life.

4. **Creative Liberation:** Often, as individuals integrate various aspects of their psyche, they experience a surge in creativity and personal expression.

The journey towards wholeness and integration in Jungian psychology is a profound process of self-discovery and transformation. It's a pathway not just to psychological health but to the realization of one's fullest potential.

12.3 The Concept of the True Self

The concept of the True Self in Jungian psychology is intricately linked to the process of individuation, representing the most authentic and integrated version of an individual. It involves the realization of one's innate potential and the harmonious unification of various aspects of the personality.

Understanding the True Self:

1. **Beyond the Persona and Ego:** The True Self is not just the persona (the social mask) or the ego (the conscious mind), but a deeper, more holistic self that encompasses both conscious and unconscious elements, including the shadow and anima/animus.

2. **The Result of Individuation:** The True Self emerges as a result of the process of individuation, where an individual integrates different parts of their psyche, leading to a state of psychological wholeness and balance.

Characteristics of the True Self:

1. **Authenticity:** The True Self is characterized by authenticity. It represents a person's genuine nature, free from the influence of societal expectations and norms.

2. **Inner Harmony and Balance:** It signifies a state of inner harmony and balance, where conflicting parts of the personality are acknowledged and integrated.

3. **Moral and Ethical Maturity:** The True Self encompasses moral and ethical maturity, reflecting deep personal values and principles.

4. **Creativity and Fulfillment:** Individuals in touch with their True Self often experience heightened creativity and a sense of fulfillment, as they are aligned with their intrinsic desires and potentials.

The Journey to the True Self:

1. **Confrontation with the Shadow:** This involves acknowledging and integrating the darker, repressed aspects of the psyche.

2. **Realization and Integration of Anima/Animus:** Understanding and harmonizing the masculine and feminine aspects within oneself is crucial in this journey.

3. **Moving Beyond the Persona:** This includes recognizing the limitations of the persona and not allowing it to dominate the personality.

4. **Continuous Process:** The realization of the True Self is not a finite goal but a continuous process of growth and self-discovery.

Implications in Therapy and Personal Development:

1. **Therapeutic Goal:** In Jungian therapy, a major goal is to help individuals discover and align with their True Self.

2. **Self-Exploration and Growth:** Techniques like dream analysis, active imagination, and exploration of personal and archetypal symbols are used to facilitate this journey.

3. **Enhanced Life Satisfaction:** Achieving closeness to the True Self is often associated with increased life satisfaction, better relationships, and a profound sense of meaning and purpose.

In conclusion, the concept of the True Self in Jungian psychology is central to the understanding of human development and potential. It represents the culmination of a person's journey towards self-realization, marked by authenticity, balance, and a deep connection with one's intrinsic nature.

12.4 Exercise: 10 MCQs with Answers at the End

1. **The True Self in Jungian psychology represents:**

   A. The social persona

   B. The conscious ego

   C. The most authentic and integrated version of an individual

   D. Only the unconscious aspects of personality

2. **The process of integrating the shadow into one's personality leads to:**

   A. Loss of personal identity

   B. Increased confusion and disorientation

   C. The realization of the True Self

   D. Weakening of the ego

3. **In Jungian psychology, encountering and integrating the Anima/Animus is crucial for:**

   A. Maintaining social norms

   B. Achieving psychological balance and self-awareness

   C. Enhancing only the intellectual capabilities

   D. Focusing on external achievements

4. **The concept of the True Self involves:**

   A. Rejecting all unconscious content

   B. Harmonious unification of conscious and unconscious elements

   C. Prioritizing societal expectations

   D. Strict adherence to logical thinking

5. **One characteristic of the True Self is:**

   A. Rigidity in beliefs and attitudes

B. Authenticity and genuine nature

C. Constant need for external validation

D. Emphasis on material success

6. **A key aspect of the journey towards the True Self includes:**

A. Avoiding emotional experiences

B. Confrontation with the Shadow

C. Suppressing creative impulses

D. Ignoring moral and ethical values

7. **In Jungian therapy, the goal of realizing the True Self is often facilitated by:**

A. Encouraging conformity to cultural norms

B. Dream analysis and active imagination

C. Focusing solely on physical health

D. Promoting competitive behaviors

8. **The True Self is associated with:**

A. Inner harmony and balance

B. Excessive focus on public image

C. Denial of personal flaws

D. Overemphasis on rationality

9. **The realization of the True Self leads to:**

A. Decreased creativity and fulfillment

B. Enhanced life satisfaction and better relationships

C. Increased dependency on others

D. Reduced ability to adapt to change

10. **The True Self in Jungian psychology is:**

A. A static, unchanging entity

B. A continuous process of growth and self-discovery

C. Only relevant in early childhood

D. Unattainable and purely theoretical

Answers

1. **C. The most authentic and integrated version of an individual**

2. **C. The realization of the True Self**

3. **B. Achieving psychological balance and self-awareness**

4. **B. Harmonious unification of conscious and unconscious elements**

5. **B. Authenticity and genuine nature**

6. **B. Confrontation with the Shadow**

7. **B. Dream analysis and active imagination**

8. **A. Inner harmony and balance**

9. **B. Enhanced life satisfaction and better relationships**

10. **B. A continuous process of growth and self-discovery**

Chapter 13: Anima and Animus

13.1 Understanding Anima and Animus

In Jungian psychology, the concepts of Anima and Animus are central to understanding the human psyche. They represent the unconscious feminine and masculine aspects present in each individual, regardless of their gender. These archetypal figures play a crucial role in how individuals relate to the opposite sex and internalize gender-related aspects.

The Anima:

1. **Feminine Aspect in Men:** The Anima is the personification of all feminine psychological tendencies in a man's psyche, such as emotions and intuitions. She is often depicted as a variety of female figures, from the seductress to the spiritual guide.

2. **Role in Men's Psyche:** The Anima influences a man's interactions with women and his attitude towards the feminine qualities within himself. She can be a source of creative inspiration and spiritual depth but also may lead to moodiness or irrational behavior if not properly integrated.

The Animus:

1. **Masculine Aspect in Women:** The Animus represents the unconscious masculine aspects in a woman's psyche. This includes qualities such as assertiveness, logic, and strength. He is often represented by a series of male figures.

2. **Influence on Women:** The Animus influences a woman's interactions with men and her feelings towards masculine qualities in herself. A well-integrated Animus contributes to inner strength and assertiveness, while an unassimilated Animus may manifest as dominating or opinionated behavior.

Integration of Anima and Animus:

1. **Achieving Balance:** Integrating the Anima and Animus involves recognizing and embracing these gendered aspects within oneself. This leads to a more balanced and holistic personality.

2. **Relationships:** Understanding and integrating these aspects can also improve relationships with the opposite sex, as it reduces projection and misunderstanding.

3. **Personal Growth:** The Anima and Animus are not static but evolve through personal development. Engaging with these aspects can lead to psychological growth and a deeper understanding of oneself.

Challenges in Integration:

1. **Projection:** One common challenge is the projection of one's Anima or Animus onto others, leading to unrealistic expectations and misunderstandings in relationships.

2. **Overidentification:** Overidentification with these archetypes can lead to stereotypical gender behaviors or an imbalance in how one relates to their own femininity or masculinity.

In Jungian psychology, the Anima and Animus are more than just concepts; they are dynamic elements of the psyche that significantly influence how individuals experience life, relationships, and their own inner world. Understanding and integrating these aspects are essential steps in achieving psychological wholeness and self-awareness.

13.2 The Role in Gender Psychology and Relationships

The concepts of Anima and Animus in Jungian psychology have profound implications for gender psychology and relationships. They provide insight into how gendered aspects of the psyche influence personality development, interpersonal dynamics, and the way individuals relate to the opposite sex.

Impact on Gender Psychology:

1. **Understanding Gendered Aspects Within:** Anima and Animus represent the internalized societal and psychological aspects of gender. Understanding these archetypes helps in exploring how gender influences one's behaviors, attitudes, and emotional responses.

2. **Influence on Gender Identity:** The integration of the Anima and Animus is significant in the development of a healthy gender identity. It allows individuals to embrace a balanced expression of masculine and feminine qualities, regardless of their biological sex.

Influence on Relationships:

1. **Projection in Romantic Relationships:** Often, individuals project their Anima or Animus onto their partners, seeing in them the qualities of their internal opposite-gender archetype. This can lead to unrealistic expectations and misinterpretations in relationships.

2. **Understanding and Communication:** Awareness of one's Anima or Animus can improve understanding and communication between partners. It helps in recognizing the projections and unconscious expectations placed on the other person.

3. **Developing Deeper Connections:** Integrating these aspects can lead to more authentic and deeper connections in

relationships, as individuals relate to each other more holistically, rather than through the lens of their projections.

Challenges and Growth in Personal Relationships:

1. **Confronting Unconscious Biases:** The journey involves confronting unconscious biases and stereotypes related to gender. This can be challenging but is essential for personal growth and healthier relationships.

2. **Maturation of Relationships:** As individuals work on integrating their Anima and Animus, their relationships often evolve. They move from being based on projection and fantasy to being grounded in reality and mutual understanding.

Therapeutic Implications:

1. **Relationship Counseling:** In therapy, understanding the dynamics of Anima and Animus can be crucial in addressing relationship issues. Therapists may explore how these archetypes influence clients' relationship patterns.

2. **Personal Development:** In individual therapy, exploring the Anima and Animus can facilitate personal development, including aspects related to gender identity, self-esteem, and emotional expression.

In conclusion, the Anima and Animus play a pivotal role in gender psychology and relationships. They offer a framework for understanding the complex interplay of gendered aspects within the psyche and how these influence personal relationships. By becoming aware of and integrating these archetypal forces, individuals can achieve greater harmony within themselves and in their interactions with others.

13.3 Balancing the Masculine and Feminine within

In Jungian psychology, the balance between the masculine (Animus) and feminine (Anima) aspects within an individual is crucial for psychological wholeness. This balance is not about gender in a biological sense but about the qualities and characteristics traditionally associated with masculinity and femininity.

Understanding Masculine and Feminine Qualities:

1. **Masculine Qualities (Animus):** Traditionally, these include logic, reason, assertiveness, and strength. In Jungian terms, a well-integrated Animus in a woman leads to a balanced use of reason and assertiveness.

2. **Feminine Qualities (Anima):** These are often associated with emotion, intuition, nurturing, and receptivity. In men, a well-integrated Anima allows for greater emotional depth and understanding.

Achieving Balance:

1. **Self-Awareness:** The first step towards balance is awareness of one's own masculine and feminine qualities. This involves recognizing how these aspects manifest in one's behavior, relationships, and self-perception.

2. **Integration of Opposites:** Balancing involves integrating the opposite gender qualities into one's personality. For instance, a man integrating his Anima learns to embrace his emotional and intuitive side, while a woman integrating her Animus might develop her assertiveness and logical thinking.

3. **Overcoming Stereotypes:** Part of the balancing process includes challenging societal and cultural stereotypes about gender. It involves allowing oneself to express traits that may not traditionally align with one's biological gender.

Implications in Personal Development:

1. **Enhanced Relationships:** A balanced integration of masculine and feminine qualities can lead to healthier and more fulfilling relationships. It enables individuals to relate to others in a more comprehensive and empathetic manner.

2. **Emotional and Psychological Growth:** Balancing these aspects contributes to emotional maturity and psychological growth. It encourages a more nuanced understanding of oneself and others.

3. **Creativity and Problem-Solving:** A balance of masculine and feminine qualities can enhance creativity and improve problem-solving skills, as it allows for a more holistic approach to challenges.

Challenges in the Process:

1. **Cultural and Personal Resistance:** There may be resistance, both culturally and personally, to embracing qualities associated with the opposite gender.

2. **Inner Conflict:** The process can initially lead to inner conflict, as it challenges deeply ingrained beliefs and behaviors.

Balancing the masculine and feminine aspects within oneself is a dynamic and ongoing process in Jungian psychology. It is not about achieving a perfect equilibrium but about recognizing and valuing the full spectrum of one's qualities and traits. This balance is key to achieving a sense of completeness and authenticity in one's life.

13.4 Exercise: 10 MCQs with Answers at the End

1. In Jungian psychology, the Anima represents:

   A. The unconscious masculine in women

B. The unconscious feminine in men

C. The collective unconscious

D. Conscious awareness in men

2. **The Animus in Jungian psychology refers to:**

A. The unconscious masculine in men

B. The unconscious feminine in women

C. The collective unconscious

D. Conscious awareness in women

3. **Balancing the Anima and Animus within oneself can lead to:**

A. Increased psychological imbalance

B. Enhanced emotional and psychological growth

C. Diminished creativity

D. Weaker problem-solving skills

4. **Projection of the Anima or Animus often affects:**

A. Financial decisions

B. Physical health

C. Romantic relationships

D. Technological abilities

5. **Integration of the Animus in a woman can result in:**

   A. Lessened logical thinking

   B. Increased assertiveness and reasoning ability

   C. Weaker emotional understanding

   D. Loss of feminine qualities

6. **A well-integrated Anima in a man contributes to:**

   A. Reduced emotional depth

   B. Greater emotional intelligence and intuition

   C. Ignorance of logic and reason

   D. Decreased creativity

7. **In Jungian therapy, exploring the Animus might help a woman:**

   A. Avoid confrontations

   B. Improve relationships with men

   C. Focus only on career development

   D. Limit her emotional expressions

8. **Challenging societal and cultural stereotypes about gender in the process of balancing the Anima and Animus involves:**

   A. Adhering strictly to traditional gender roles

B. Expressing traits traditionally associated with the opposite biological gender

C. Avoiding any traits associated with the opposite gender

D. Focusing on physical attributes rather than psychological traits

9. The Anima and Animus are considered part of the:

A. Personal unconscious

B. Conscious mind

C. Ego

D. Collective unconscious

10. A key challenge in integrating the Anima and Animus is:

A. Cultural and personal resistance to embracing opposite gender qualities

B. Excessive focus on physical strength

C. Loss of individual identity

D. Overemphasis on rationality over emotion

Answers

1. **B. The unconscious feminine in men**

2. **A. The unconscious masculine in women**

3. **B. Enhanced emotional and psychological growth**

4. **C. Romantic relationships**

5. **B. Increased assertiveness and reasoning ability**

6. **B. Greater emotional intelligence and intuition**

7. **B. Improve relationships with men**

8. **B. Expressing traits traditionally associated with the opposite biological gender**

9. **A. Personal unconscious**

10. **A. Cultural and personal resistance to embracing opposite gender qualities**

Chapter 14: Synchronicity and the Unexplained

14.1 The Principle of Synchronicity

Carl Jung introduced the concept of synchronicity, a principle that has intrigued both psychologists and those interested in the intersection of psychology and spirituality. Synchronicity refers to the occurrence of meaningful coincidences that seem to have no causal relationship but are deeply significant to the individuals experiencing them.

Understanding Synchronicity:

1. **Acausal Connecting Principle:** Synchronicity is described by Jung as an "acausal connecting principle," where events are connected not by causality but by meaning. This concept challenges the conventional scientific understanding that every effect has a direct cause.

2. **Meaningful Coincidences:** Synchronicity occurs when an external event coincides with a psychological state or process, and this coincidence holds significant personal meaning. For example, thinking about a specific, uncommon subject and then encountering it unexpectedly in an unrelated context.

3. **Link to the Unconscious:** Jung believed synchronicity might reveal something important from the unconscious. It can provide insight, guidance, or affirmation related to a person's internal thoughts, emotions, or life situation.

Implications of Synchronicity:

1. **Personal Insight and Growth:** Experiences of synchronicity can lead to personal insights and growth. They may prompt individuals to explore aspects of their lives or psyche that they have not previously considered.

2. **Spiritual and Psychological Significance:** Synchronicity often holds spiritual or psychological significance for those who experience it, leading them to contemplate deeper aspects of existence and their own place within it.

3. **Exploration of the Unconscious:** In therapy, discussions about synchronistic events can be valuable for exploring unconscious processes, beliefs, and emotions.

Challenges and Criticisms:

1. **Scientific Skepticism:** Synchronicity challenges traditional scientific views of causality and is often met with skepticism by the scientific community.

2. **Subjectivity:** The highly personal and subjective nature of synchronistic experiences makes them difficult to study or validate objectively.

Jung's Perspective on Synchronicity:

1. **Beyond Causality:** Jung viewed synchronicity as a phenomenon that extends beyond the limitations of cause and effect, suggesting a more interconnected and meaningful universe.

2. **Integration of Science and Spirituality:** Synchronicity represents Jung's effort to bridge the gap between the scientific understanding of the world and the realm of the spiritual or unexplained.

In summary, the principle of synchronicity in Jungian psychology points to a world where meaningful connections occur beyond the scope of causality. It represents a confluence of the external and internal worlds, where the boundaries between the psychological and the physical blur, offering profound and often inexplicable insights into our lives and experiences.

14.2 Case Studies and Examples

The concept of synchronicity in Jungian psychology is best illustrated through case studies and examples. These instances demonstrate how seemingly unrelated events can coincide in a meaningful way, providing insights or highlighting underlying psychological processes.

Example 1: The Scarab Beetle

One of the most famous case studies cited by Jung involves a patient who was recounting a dream she had about a golden scarab. At that moment, an insect hit the window of Jung's office. Upon examining it, Jung found it to be a scarabaeid beetle, a close analog to the golden scarab in the patient's dream. This synchronistic event helped break through the patient's rational skepticism and facilitated a breakthrough in her therapy.

Example 2: The Book and The Dream

Another example involves a patient who dreamt of a "monograph" (a detailed written study) on a certain biological species. The next day, without prior knowledge of this dream, Jung handed the patient a monograph on the same species. This meaningful coincidence led to significant therapeutic insights for the patient.

Example 3: The Lost Watch

In a personal anecdote, Jung wrote about a time when he had lost his watch, a prized possession. He searched for it unsuccessfully and eventually resigned himself to its loss. Some time later, during a period of emotional distress, he found the watch in an unexpected place. For Jung, the timing of the rediscovery was deeply meaningful and synchronistic, coinciding with a moment of psychological significance.

Example 4: The Chilling Forecast

Another case involved a patient who dreamt of being in a mountainous region where she saw a heavy downpour that turned into a flood, causing massive destruction. The next day, a dam broke in that very region, causing a flood similar to what the patient had dreamt.

Interpretation of Synchronistic Events:

1. **Reflecting the Unconscious:** These events are often seen as reflections or manifestations of the unconscious mind, revealing inner thoughts, conflicts, or preoccupations.

2. **Therapeutic Insights:** In therapy, synchronistic events can provide valuable insights. They can be used to explore the patient's feelings, thoughts, and internal conflicts.

3. **Personal Meaning:** The significance of synchronistic events is highly personal. The meaning derived from these occurrences can vary greatly depending on the individual's situation and psychological state.

These case studies and examples demonstrate how synchronicity can play a role in both everyday life and therapeutic settings. They highlight Jung's view that our inner and outer worlds are deeply connected and that meaningful coincidences can provide valuable insights into our psyche and life journey.

14.3 Implications for Understanding Reality

Carl Jung's concept of synchronicity has profound implications for understanding reality, challenging conventional perceptions of causality and the nature of the universe. This principle suggests that there is more to reality than what can be explained by cause-and-effect relationships, pointing towards a deeper, more interconnected and meaningful existence.

Expanding the Concept of Reality:

1. **Acausal Connections:** Synchronicity introduces the idea of acausal connections, where events are linked not by cause and effect but through meaning. This expands the traditional scientific understanding of how events relate to each other.

2. **Interplay of Conscious and Unconscious:** Synchronicity suggests that the unconscious mind can interact with the external world in meaningful ways, blurring the lines between subjective and objective reality.

Psychological and Spiritual Dimensions:

1. **Inner and Outer World Connection:** The principle of synchronicity implies a deep connection between the inner world of the psyche and the outer physical world. It suggests that our inner thoughts, emotions, and unconscious processes can manifest in external events.

2. **Spiritual and Mystical Insights:** Synchronicity often carries a spiritual or mystical significance for those who experience it, leading to a sense of wonder and a deeper consideration of spiritual dimensions of existence.

Implications for Science and Philosophy:

1. **Challenge to Scientific Materialism:** Synchronicity challenges the materialistic worldview that dominates much of science, suggesting that there are aspects of reality that cannot be explained solely through physical processes.

2. **New Frameworks of Understanding:** It invites the development of new philosophical and scientific frameworks that acknowledge the role of consciousness and meaning in the fabric of reality.

Therapeutic Implications:

1. **Enhanced Therapeutic Practice:** In psychotherapy, synchronicity can be a valuable tool for uncovering unconscious material and facilitating personal insights, enriching the therapeutic process.

2. **Holistic Approach to Mental Health:** It supports a more holistic approach to mental health, recognizing the interconnectedness of psychological, physical, and spiritual dimensions.

Personal and Societal Impact:

1. **Personal Growth:** Individuals who experience synchronicity often report profound personal growth, increased self-awareness, and a reassessment of their life's meaning and purpose.

2. **Cultural Shift:** The acceptance and understanding of synchronicity can lead to a cultural shift towards a more integrated view of reality that values both the rational and the mystical.

In summary, the implications of synchronicity for understanding reality are far-reaching. It challenges us to think beyond conventional boundaries and consider a more interconnected and meaningful universe where the inner workings of the mind are inextricably linked to the external world.

14.4 Exercise: 10 MCQs with Answers at the End

1. Carl Jung's concept of synchronicity refers to:

A. The process of aging

B. Meaningful coincidences that are not causally related

C. Random events with no significance

D. Traditional cause-and-effect relationships

2. Synchronicity challenges the traditional scientific view of:

A. Artistic creativity

B. Emotional intelligence

C. Cause and effect

D. Technological advancement

3. In synchronistic events, the connection between events is based on:

A. Physical proximity

B. Temporal sequence

C. Shared meaning

D. Genetic similarity

4. Jung's concept of synchronicity expands our understanding of reality by introducing:

A. Acausal connecting principles

B. The importance of chronological order

C. The irrelevance of human consciousness

D. The supremacy of physical laws

5. **One implication of synchronicity for psychotherapy is:**

A. Decreased emphasis on the unconscious

B. Enhanced understanding of unconscious material

C. Focus on pharmaceutical treatments

D. Discouragement of personal insight

6. **Synchronicity in Jungian psychology suggests a deep connection between:**

A. Different cultural practices

B. Inner psychological processes and external events

C. Various biological systems

D. Economic factors and personal wealth

7. **An example of a synchronistic event could be:**

A. Winning a lottery

B. Thinking of an old friend and then unexpectedly meeting them

C. Experiencing a natural disaster

D. Learning a new language

8. The spiritual or mystical significance of synchronicity leads to:

A. A sense of confusion

B. Increased materialism

C. A deeper consideration of spiritual dimensions

D. A focus on physical health

9. For someone experiencing synchronicity, it often results in:

A. Profound personal growth and self-awareness

B. Decreased curiosity about the world

C. A heightened sense of fear

D. Lessened importance of personal experiences

10. In Jungian psychology, synchronicity is seen as a challenge to:

A. Artistic expression

B. Scientific materialism

C. Historical analysis

D. Linguistic development

Answers

1. **B. Meaningful coincidences that are not causally related**

2. **C. Cause and effect**

3. **C. Shared meaning**

4. **A. Acausal connecting principles**

5. **B. Enhanced understanding of unconscious material**

6. **B. Inner psychological processes and external events**

7. **B. Thinking of an old friend and then unexpectedly meeting them**

8. **C. A deeper consideration of spiritual dimensions**

9. **A. Profound personal growth and self-awareness**

10. **B. Scientific materialism**

Chapter 15: Jung's Legacy and Future Directions

15.1 The Continuing Impact of Jungian Psychology

Carl Jung's contributions to psychology have created a lasting impact, influencing not only the field of psychology but also extending into areas like art, literature, spirituality, and even popular culture. His concepts continue to inspire and challenge, offering a rich framework for understanding the human psyche.

Enduring Influence in Various Fields:

1. **Depth Psychology:** Jung's ideas form the foundation of depth psychology, emphasizing the exploration of the unconscious and its influence on behavior and personality.

2. **Psychotherapy:** Jungian analysis remains a distinct and influential approach in psychotherapy, focusing on the process of individuation, dream interpretation, and the integration of the shadow.

3. **Art and Literature:** Jung's exploration of symbols, archetypes, and the collective unconscious continues to influence artists,

writers, and filmmakers, enriching the way stories and artworks are interpreted and created.

4. **Spirituality and Religion:** Jung's ideas about the spiritual dimensions of the human experience have found resonance in modern spiritual practices and have bridged the gap between psychology and spirituality.

Jung's Concepts in Contemporary Psychology:

1. **Complexes and Archetypes:** These continue to be relevant in understanding personality and human behavior. They provide a lens for exploring deep-seated emotional patterns and collective human themes.

2. **The Unconscious Mind:** Jung's view of the unconscious as a dynamic, influential part of the psyche is integral to many modern psychological theories and therapeutic practices.

3. **Synchronicity:** This concept challenges conventional notions of causality and has sparked discussions in both psychology and physics about the nature of reality.

Challenges and Criticisms:

1. **Scientific Validity:** Some of Jung's concepts, particularly those relating to the collective unconscious and archetypes, face criticism for lacking empirical support.

2. **Cultural and Historical Context:** Jung's ideas are sometimes critiqued for being reflective of their cultural and historical context, necessitating reinterpretation or adaptation for modern applicability.

Future Directions and Adaptations:

1. **Integration with New Psychological Theories:** There is ongoing work to integrate Jung's ideas with newer psychological theories, such as those in cognitive psychology, neurology, and evolutionary psychology.

2. **Holistic and Interdisciplinary Approach:** Jung's holistic approach to understanding the human psyche is increasingly relevant in an interdisciplinary world, where the intersection of psychology with other disciplines offers new insights.

3. **Global and Cultural Adaptation:** Jung's concepts are being re-examined and adapted to fit diverse cultural contexts, recognizing the universality of some experiences and the specificity of others.

In summary, Carl Jung's legacy continues to be a powerful force in psychology and beyond. His insights into the human psyche have enduring relevance, offering tools for personal growth, understanding human behavior, and exploring the deeper aspects of existence. As psychology continues to evolve, Jung's ideas will likely be revisited, reinterpreted, and integrated in new and innovative ways.

15.2 Jungian Psychology in the 21st Century

As we move through the 21st century, Jungian psychology remains a vibrant and evolving field, adapting to contemporary challenges and integrating with modern psychological research and practice. The relevance of Jung's ideas in today's world is seen in various areas, from clinical psychology to cultural studies.

Adaptation to Modern Contexts:

1. **Integration with Neuroscience:** There's a growing interest in exploring the connections between Jung's theories and neuroscience, particularly in understanding how archetypes and the collective unconscious might be represented in the brain.

2. **Digital and Virtual Realities:** The rise of digital and virtual realities offers new avenues for exploring Jungian concepts like persona and shadow, as individuals navigate and construct identities in virtual spaces.

3. **Addressing Global Challenges:** Jungian psychology is being applied to understand and address global issues like environmental crises, cultural conflicts, and societal changes, using its insights to foster a deeper understanding of collective human behavior.

Jungian Psychology in Therapy:

1. **Holistic and Individual Approaches:** Jungian therapy continues to offer a holistic approach that addresses the individual needs and journey of each client, focusing on self-realization and integration.

2. **Diversity and Inclusivity:** Modern Jungian practitioners are increasingly focusing on incorporating diverse cultural perspectives and ensuring that Jung's concepts are applicable and respectful across different cultural contexts.

3. **Online and Remote Therapy:** The adaptation of Jungian therapy to online platforms has made it more accessible to a wider audience, allowing for the exploration of the psyche in new and flexible formats.

Jung's Ideas in Culture and Society:

1. **Pop Culture and Media:** Jungian archetypes and themes are prevalent in movies, literature, and other media, providing a rich framework for storytelling and character development.

2. **Public Discourse and Education:** Jung's concepts are often used in discussions about societal trends, political movements, and educational philosophies, highlighting their enduring relevance.

Challenges and Future Directions:

1. **Reconciling with Empirical Science:** One of the main challenges for Jungian psychology is integrating its concepts with empirical scientific research, ensuring its methods and theories are validated and refined.

2. **Adapting to Social Changes:** As societal norms and understandings of identity, gender, and culture evolve, Jungian psychology will need to adapt its concepts to remain relevant and sensitive to these changes.

In the 21st century, Jungian psychology continues to offer valuable insights into the human psyche, providing tools for personal growth and understanding of collective phenomena. Its future lies in its ability to adapt, integrate with other disciplines, and respond to the changing landscape of human society and culture.

15.3 Future Trends and Potential Developments

As Jungian psychology moves forward in the 21st century, it is poised to evolve in response to new scientific discoveries, cultural shifts, and societal needs. Several trends and potential developments are likely to shape the future of this field.

1. Integration with Neuroscience and Technology:

- **Brain Research:** Advances in neuroscience could provide empirical support for Jungian concepts like archetypes and the collective unconscious. Exploring how these ideas manifest in brain activity and structure is a potential area of development.

- **Virtual Reality (VR) and Artificial Intelligence (AI):** The use of VR and AI in therapy, including Jungian therapy, could provide innovative ways to explore the psyche, dreams, and unconscious processes.

2. Globalization and Cross-Cultural Perspectives:

- **Incorporating Diverse Cultural Contexts:** As the world becomes more interconnected, Jungian psychology will likely incorporate more diverse cultural and spiritual perspectives, enriching its understanding of the human psyche.

- **Addressing Global Challenges:** Jungian concepts could be applied to understand and address global issues like climate change, cultural conflicts, and migration, offering insights into collective human behavior.

3. Personalized and Online Therapies:

- **Tailored Therapeutic Approaches:** There will be a continued emphasis on personalizing therapy to individual needs, possibly using AI and data analysis to tailor Jungian therapeutic techniques.

- **Expansion of Online Therapy:** The accessibility of Jungian therapy will likely increase through online platforms, making it available to a broader audience.

4. Ecological and Environmental Psychology:

- **Eco-psychology:** Jungian psychology could intersect with eco-psychology, exploring the relationship between the human psyche and the natural world, and addressing the psychological aspects of environmental crises.

5. Educational and Developmental Applications:

- **Education Systems:** Jung's ideas might be increasingly applied in educational settings, offering insights into child development, learning processes, and creativity.

6. Evolving Understanding of Identity and Consciousness:

- **Gender and Sexuality:** As societal understandings of gender and sexuality evolve, Jungian psychology will adapt its concepts of anima and animus, and explore new dimensions of identity.

- **Expanded Concepts of Consciousness:** Ongoing philosophical and scientific discussions about consciousness could lead to new theories within Jungian psychology, expanding its scope and depth.

7. Interdisciplinary Collaborations:

- **Collaboration with Other Fields:** Jungian psychology is likely to engage more with other disciplines, such as anthropology, sociology, and philosophy, to deepen its insights and expand its applicability.

In summary, the future of Jungian psychology is dynamic and promising, with potential developments spanning from technological integration to global and environmental applications. These advancements will likely enrich the field, making it more relevant, inclusive, and effective in addressing the complexities of modern human experience.

15.4 Exercise: 10 MCQs with Answers at the End

1. **Future developments in Jungian psychology may involve integration with:**

   A. Neuroscience

   B. Mathematics

   C. Economics

   D. Political science

2. **The use of virtual reality (VR) in Jungian therapy could help in:**

   A. Replacing traditional therapy methods

   B. Exploring the psyche and unconscious processes

   C. Focusing solely on physical health

   D. Enhancing financial management skills

3. **Incorporating diverse cultural perspectives in Jungian psychology can lead to:**

A. Diminished relevance in therapy

B. A richer understanding of the human psyche

C. Overemphasis on technology

D. Reduced emphasis on personal growth

4. **The application of Jungian concepts to global issues like climate change reflects:**

A. A departure from Jung's original ideas

B. A misunderstanding of psychological principles

C. The adaptability of Jungian psychology to contemporary challenges

D. An overextension of psychological theories

5. **Online platforms for Jungian therapy are likely to:**

A. Decrease the effectiveness of therapy

B. Make therapy accessible to a broader audience

C. Limit the scope of Jungian concepts

D. Focus exclusively on younger generations

6. **Jungian psychology's intersection with eco-psychology is centered on:**

A. The economic impact of environmental policies

B. The relationship between the human psyche and the natural world

C. Technological solutions to environmental issues

D. Political strategies for conservation

7. **In education, Jungian concepts might be used to:**

A. Enforce strict behavioral standards

B. Provide insights into child development and learning processes

C. Discourage creativity and imagination

D. Promote competitive academic environments

8. **Adaptations in Jungian psychology regarding gender and sexuality are likely due to:**

A. Changes in medical practices

B. Evolving societal understandings of identity

C. Shifts in global economic trends

D. Advances in computer technology

9. **Interdisciplinary collaborations in Jungian psychology could involve:**

   A. Abandoning psychological principles

   B. Engaging with fields like anthropology and sociology

   C. Focusing solely on historical research

   D. Limiting its scope to psychological analysis

10. **The expansion of Jungian psychology in the 21st century is characterized by:**

   A. Resistance to change and new ideas

   B. A dynamic and evolving approach to modern challenges

   C. A return to traditional 19th-century practices

   D. An exclusive focus on Jung's original teachings

Answers

1. **A. Neuroscience**

2. **B. Exploring the psyche and unconscious processes**

3. **B. A richer understanding of the human psyche**

4. **C. The adaptability of Jungian psychology to contemporary challenges**

5. **B.** Make therapy accessible to a broader audience

6. **B.** The relationship between the human psyche and the natural world

7. **B.** Provide insights into child development and learning processes

8. **B.** Evolving societal understandings of identity

9. **B.** Engaging with fields like anthropology and sociology

10. **B.** A dynamic and evolving approach to modern challenges

Conclusion

As we conclude our exploration of Jungian psychology, it's clear that Carl Jung's legacy extends far beyond the boundaries of traditional psychology. His theories on the unconscious, archetypes, individuation, the shadow, anima and animus, and synchronicity have provided a rich framework for understanding the depth and complexity of the human psyche. Jungian psychology offers valuable insights into personal growth, creativity, spiritual development, and the interconnectedness of our inner and outer worlds.

Key Takeaways:

1. **Depth of the Unconscious:** Jung's exploration of the unconscious has emphasized its profound impact on behavior, thoughts, and emotional life.

2. **The Process of Individuation:** The journey towards psychological wholeness and self-realization is central to Jung's work, emphasizing the importance of integrating various aspects of the psyche.

3. **Cultural and Spiritual Dimensions:** Jungian psychology bridges the gap between psychology and spirituality, acknowledging the importance of cultural and spiritual dimensions in personal development.

4. **Contemporary Relevance:** Despite being a product of its time, Jungian psychology continues to evolve and adapt, maintaining its relevance in the modern world by addressing contemporary issues and integrating with new scientific developments.

5. **Interdisciplinary Influence:** Jung's ideas have influenced a wide range of fields, from art and literature to religious studies and environmental psychology.

Future Directions:

Jungian psychology will continue to evolve, integrating with disciplines like neuroscience, embracing technological advancements, and adapting to cultural changes. It will likely remain a significant source of insight for understanding the human condition and addressing the psychological needs of individuals and societies.

In summary, Carl Jung's contributions to psychology have created a lasting legacy that continues to inspire, challenge, and guide those on a journey of self-discovery and those seeking a deeper understanding of the human experience. As we move forward, his ideas will undoubtedly continue to influence and inform our understanding of the intricate tapestry of the human mind and its place in the broader tapestry of life.

The best way to thank an author is to

write a review.